Greatham Memories

Dedicated to the memory of Shirley and Pat Redpath

by Peter Gripton

Greatham Memories

"Unless we know about the past, we will remain forever children. For what is the worth of human life, unless it is woven into the lives of our ancestors by the study of history?"

Cicero

First Edition 2008 by Las Atalayas Publishing

Author and Editor Peter Gripton
Copyright © Peter Gripton 2008

The moral rights of the author have been asserted. All rights reserved. No part of this publication may be reproduced, stored in a retrieval system or transmitted in any form or by any means, electronic, mechanical or otherwise without the written permission of the Publisher.

ISBN 978-0-9556753-4-8

Design and Typesetting by kenandglen.com

Acknowledgements

My most grateful thanks go to all those kindly people, both inside and outside **Greatham**, who have contributed their stories, memories and photographs to this publication. Their names appear below and I apologise for any omissions - if there are any, they were certainly not intentional.

Beenham, Chris	Blackwell, 'Betty'	Booton, Alan
Cooke, John	Duffet, Paul	Dunn, Brenda
Fisher, Julia	Flack, Pat and Ray	Ford, Michael
Foster, Nigel	Graves, John	Jenkinson, Huguette
Lockley, Julie	Marie, Bill	Redman, David
Redman, Olive	Redpath, Mark	Rolling, Jane
Sammonds, Charles	Shotter, Ron	Sillence, Simon
Siney, Alan	Spratt, Hugh	Swatton, Prue
Wells, Ray	Workman, Phyllis	

About the author

On October 31st 2007, my wife Joyce and I celebrated forty years of living at Chapel House in **Greatham**. I guess one could now say that we have completed our trial period and now qualify for residential status! When I first came into the village, it was at the invitation of George Armitage of New House, which adjoins Chapel House, forming a pair of semi-detached houses. George was then a Supervising Instructor at the School of Electrical and Mechanical Engineering (SEME) up at Bordon, where I had myself just started work as a Civilian Instructional Officer. Settling next door to George certainly came in handy. Not only were we able to share the ten-minute drive to work, but he was technically excellent in the repair of cars – or 'old bangers' – of which I became the owner of quite a few! George was a 'hands on' type and owned a vast range of tools and equipment that he was only too ready to share. Sadly, he passed away in 1988, but I will always remember him, not only as a great mechanic, but also as a good friend and neighbour.

The publication of my book, *'A History of Greatham'*, back in 2003, came almost as a great shock to me, considering that I knew virtually nothing of the village or its history when I settled here! I had certainly never set out with the intention of 'writing a book', but when the opportunity arose, it gave me great pleasure to assemble all those facts and figures, as well as the 'human interest' stories, that came my way from so many helpful sources. Since then, with the book having been widely circulated outside the **Greatham** environment, it has been really nice to communicate with those people who had received copies and then been prepared to share their own memories of living in the village. It is this enthusiasm and interest from outside that has pushed me into putting together this collection of *'Greatham Memories'*. As for myself, it has been quite sad to recall that many contributors to my first book have since departed this mortal life – May and George Lockley, Charlie Hanson, George Wakeford and Ray Jenkinson, to name but a few.

Having served as an 'Apprentice Soldier' at Arborfield, between 1956 and 1959, it is with much pride and pleasure that I am now 'the editor' of the Arborfield Old Boys' Association Newsletter, which is published three times every year. This gives me the chance to converse with other such ex-Apprentices from all over the world, taking their stories and photographs and putting them into print, in much the same manner as for this book. There's never a dull moment! Finally, I must pay tribute to my wife Joyce, who puts up with my 'dabbling on the computer' with great perseverance – as she says, *"It keeps him out of mischief!"*

Contents

Chapter 1	Forestside Farm	1
Chapter 2	The Redman Family	3
Chapter 3	Julia Fisher	13
Chapter 4	Captain Augustus Coryton	15
Chapter 5	Deal Farm	18
Chapter 6	Lady Anne Brewis	22
Chapter 7	Old Chapel	24
Chapter 8	Paul Duffett	26
Chapter 9	Jane Coombes	29
Chapter 10	Keepers Cottage	35
Chapter 11	Phyllis Workman	38
Chapter 12	Greatham Mill Gardens	46
Chapter 13	John Cooke	48
Chapter 14	Jack Dunn	50
Chapter 15	Pilgrims Way	60
Chapter 16	Shotter Family	63
Chapter 17	Win Murphy	64
Chapter 18	The Foster Connection	65
Chapter 19	Greatham Allotments	68
Chapter 20	Greatham Service Station	70
Chapter 21	The Jenkinsons	74
Chapter 22	The Leggett Legacy	79
Chapter 23	The Redpaths	81
Chapter 24	Heathland Project	84
Chapter 25	Greatham Inn	85
Chapter 26	The Carylls	86
Epilogue		89
Appendix A	Le Court	90
Appendix B	Manor House	91
Appendix C	Pubs and Hotels	92
Index		94

Foreword

When I had my book '*A History of Greatham*' published in late 2003, little did I think that I would ever be writing the 'foreword' to another book concerning **Greatham**. But, during the past four years, many people far and wide have sent me further contributions, ones that they said they were quite happy to share with local inhabitants. The accompanying articles and stories cannot in any way be described as '*A History of Greatham Part 2*', but I hope that readers will enjoy them just the same.

Alan Siney

Those who have read the original book will recognise the name of Alan Siney as one of its main contributors. Alan was brought up in **Greatham**, along with his brothers Don and Eric, and has long and fond memories of them all growing up in our Hampshire village. Alan kindly sent this letter, which I have great pleasure in sharing with readers.

*"I was fascinated by Pete Gripton's '**A History of Greatham**' and must congratulate him for persevering and achieving this great effort of his, especially as the parish is a relatively small subject, giving rise to financial and feasibility doubts. The resultant success of the book is what he deserves and, upon receiving it, I found it hard to put down and finished reading it in a couple of days.*

I must apologise to Pete for the fact that my contribution was hurriedly submitted and only after his initial draft had been completed – which must have delayed its production and caused him a few headaches. My excuse for failing to act sooner was because of my own involvement with research and writing, in relation to my own area and County of West Sussex. This also precluded me from conducting further research in the Hampshire County Archives, although my one visit to Winchester in 1987 did provide a useful background to mid-19th century tithes and landholdings.

*Sixty or so years ago, we were 'outdoor' beings and **Greatham** was our domain; largely thanks to the liberality of Captain Coryton in allowing us to roam freely over his land as if ours by right. It was a good arrangement; he respected our freedom and we respected his crops; thus allowing those inveterate wanderers so inclined to intimately know the parish and its far-flung aspects.*

*The book brought sharply to mind so many old '**Greathamites**', some well remembered and others almost forgotten – but recalled through the mists of time. It gives great satisfaction to know that this history of **Greatham**, and those that contributed to its ever-changing lifestyle, will always be recorded for future generations, as brought to fruition by Pete's good work.*

With sincere good wishes, Alan Siney, Rudgwick, W.Sussex, Feb 4th 2004.

Alan's literate contribution, via his cousin Elsie (Collins) did very much catch me on the hop! When I first received his typewritten document, it must have been about fifty pages worth and I had many doubts as to whether or not I could include it. But, having read through his amazing memoirs and the detail therein contained, I made sure that it was all included in the final book. I am sure that all who have read Alan's contribution will recognise his special talents at describing a **Greatham** that has long since almost disappeared. For anyone who hasn't read the book, Alan's story alone is well worth the admission fee!

Charles Sammonds

I was most surprised to accept a telephone call one morning in late October 2003, requesting a copy of my book '*A History of Greatham*'. After all, the van-load of books had only arrived at my house the previous evening – and this call was coming from Wolverhampton, situated up in what is known as 'the Black Country'! However, all was explained when the caller turned out to be Charles Sammonds, known to many locals as an evacuee to nearby Empshott back in 1939. Charles is a regular subscriber to our Parish Magazine and obviously gets his copy before most of the local population! He had read my first notification of the forthcoming issue of the history and was eager to receive a copy, post haste.

Unfortunately, Charles appears not to have enjoyed the best of health in recent years and is unable, at present, to travel far from his home in the 'Black Country'. He was, however, able to pen a few lines to me, in gratitude for my sending him a book so promptly. I am sure he will not mind me letting you share a few of his thoughts from the letter that he sent, which appear next:

"Congratulations on the book – a wonderful effort, full of nostalgic information and evocative situations. My wife has berated me for sitting down with it when I ought to have been wiping up, but, once I caught sight of a name I knew, I just had to follow it through.

Although I am slowly recovering from my heart attacks, at present it seems that I shall not be able to travel any distance. It grieves me to think that I am unable to rejoice in the beautiful countryside of Hampshire, but the Parish Magazine keeps me informed and now your book has given me some wonderfully nostalgic information and pictures. If only someone would write the history of Empshott in the same way!"

Thank you for your letter Charles, I have never met you personally, but I feel that I know you well through the two letters I have received from you. I hope that you will continue to gain pleasure from the monthly magazine and, who knows, maybe someone from Empshott will take up the challenge!

(Postscript: the above was written towards the end of 2003, since when I understand that Charles has sadly passed away.)

I do hope readers do not mind me including the above two letters in what is a 'Foreword', but they provide a convenient link between my original book and this one.

Peter Gripton, October 2007.

Chapter 1
Forestside Farm

Early in 2005, I received an e-mail that read as follows:

"I would like to purchase a copy of your book 'A History of Greatham'. Please can you let me know if it is still available, how much I should make my cheque out for and to whom it should be made payable to and where to send.

Thanks, Michael Ford."

I replied and sent off a copy of the book right away and asked Michael from where he had developed his interest in **Greatham** and its history, to which he immediately responded:

*"Thanks for your prompt reply. I will put a cheque in the post for you tomorrow. My current interest in **Greatham** is because of my research into the churches and chapels of Hampshire. I have found that local historians are one of the best sources of the information that I am looking for.*

*However, I also have a genealogical interest in the area, as William Ford, a younger brother of my great-great-great grandfather, farmed Forestside Farm on the Farnham Road at Blackmoor in Victorian times. He married a Mary Blanchard in 1825 and their first two children were baptised at Empshott, while the remaining five were all baptised at **Greatham Church**.*

*I look forward to reading your book and finding out more about **Greatham**.*

Regards, Michael."

Forestside Farm today, present home to the Redman family

It is immensely pleasing to know that interest in the local history of the area is still strong and that my book is becoming a source of reference! Michael duly received his copy and wrote back to thank me, adding that he had found my details on the *'Southern Life'* web-site.

I was delighted, just a few days after Michael had last written to me, to receive another letter, containing the last will and testament of David Ford, son of the aforementioned William Ford. It was also surprising to find that David Ford's will was constructed in 1888, whilst his father was still very much alive! David bequeathed his estate, to be divided equally between his brother George Ford and two sisters, Mary Ann Teague and Fanny Darby. This was on the condition that, should David predecease his father, his three siblings should contribute 'in an equal degree' towards their father's maintenance. Later, in 1900, the self-same will was attested with the information that George Ford had been granted the estate, which at that time had a gross value of £338. 17s. 6d.

I showed the above information to Olive Redman, still living at Forestside Farm with her son David, and she told me that Edgar (her husband, who died in early 2004) used to talk about 'Farmer Ford'. She also thought that the place used to be called 'Ford Farm' at one time, though she has no documentation to that effect. But I find myself consistently amazed at how these small threads of history are so inter-woven together.

Chapter 2
The Redman family

On the morning of Wednesday 21st April 2004, members of family, along with many friends, neighbours and acquaintances, gathered together at St John's Church to bid farewell to one of *Greatham's* oldest and best known inhabitants. Edgar Redman had died just a few days previously, at the end of a long and fruitful life. As befitting such a sombre occasion, the day itself arrived with totally overcast grey skies, continual drizzly rain and a moderately cold wind. Unfortunately, Edgar had spent his latter years suffering from what has become the 'modern curse' of Alzheimer's Disease, an affliction that savagely robs a person of much of his or her memories. And so, despite the obvious sadness of the event, Olive and son David must have felt a profound sense of relief that Edgar's long battle with the illness had now been brought to a peaceful and dignified end.

Those who knew Edgar Redman from his earliest days would remember him, in the main, as a 'country gentleman, farmer and dairyman' – and these facts were duly spelled out by the Reverend David Heatley during his funeral address. Towards the end of the service, when the congregation stood to sing the final hymn, the Rector said that people might wonder what was the connection between Edgar and a 'life at sea'. He then went on to explain that the hymn, *"Eternal Father, strong to save"*, with its poignant line *"For those in peril on the sea"*, had long been one of Edgar's favourites. After the interment, most people stayed on in the church room afterwards at the request of Olive and family, during which time many tales of Edgar's life and achievements were swapped over tea and sandwiches.

Edgar Redman

Edgar was born here in *Greatham* during 1914, the year that also saw the outbreak of the First World War. He was the second son of William Albert and Emma Jane Redman, born at their home in Rook's Farm, on the Petersfield Road. As would be expected in those undoubtedly simpler times, he initially attended the village school and would have been a pupil during the time of two different Headmasters, firstly Charles Hiscock up

Edgar Redman at home circa 1995

Blackmoor Village Hall once the village school attended by Olive Redman

until 1920-1921, followed by Charles Jeffery Wain, who then remained at **Greatham School** right through until 1944.

Both Edgar and his older sibling, William, went on to attend prestigious Churcher's College, just a few miles south of **Greatham**, in the bustling market town of Petersfield. Upon leaving Churcher's, Edgar started out on his life's task as a countryman, working on the family dairy farm, no doubt herding the cattle and tending the chickens, before delivering milk, butter and eggs around the local area, much as his father had done before him. He would have been a familiar sight around both the village and the nearby Longmoor Army Camp, as he did his daily rounds.

One lady villager once told the tale of once being disturbed by the sound of 'heavy breathing' behind her, as she sat resting in the kitchen of her home. Fortunately, it turned out to be merely one of the cows that had escaped from Edgar's custody! Because of his 'reserved occupation', when World War II broke out in 1939, Edgar was no doubt relieved not to be called up for active service. Instead he went on to become a member of the local Home Guard – the *'Dad's Army'* of television comedy fame – as well as working for Lord Selborne on the nearby Blackmoor Estate.

Edgar and William had always been exceptionally talented in terms of a musical background. Indeed, William – or Will, as he was usually known – Redman was the Church organist here at **Greatham** for over sixty years, while Edgar was a long-time member of the choir and also served on the Parochial Church Council. His fine tenor voice could often be heard assisting the Hawkley and Liss Choral Societies. Also a talented flautist, Edgar played for the Liss Light Orchestra during the Fifties and lent his musical abilities to many a *Gilbert and Sullivan* production. Indeed, a newspaper article dating from 1952 announced that the Liss Guild was in the middle of a three-day run of its annual variety show in St Mary's Hall. Apart from the violinists, there were a certain *"E Redman on flute and W Redman on clarinet"*, while the whole show was described as *"one of the best yet"*.

Edgar marries Olive

At the age of forty-five years, Edgar married Olive Bridger in 1959, here at the church in **Greatham**. The Rev R W Tyler, who was by then Rector of both **Greatham** and Empshott, administered the wedding service. The Redman's only son and heir, David, was born later the same year. *(In my book, 'A History of Greatham', I indicated that David was born in 1960, but that was actually the year of his baptism, as denoted in the Parish Register. Ed.)* As with many country people, the farm was Edgar's life and he never really had what could be termed a holiday. When not actually working on the farm, he could be found out in the fresh air, tending the garden, which was always his pride and joy.

He was a loving family man, devoted to his wife and son; honest, hard working and conscientious, he had a firm eye for detail, which could prove to be pretty infuriating on occasion. He loved his home at Forestside Farm, having moved there in 1962, following a spell in Benham's Lane. At the time, both Edgar's father and brother were also living on the farm, a state of affairs that lasted just

*Olive and Edgar married at **Greatham** in February 1959*

a couple of years, as Mr W A Redman died in 1964, at the age of some eighty-one years. Elder brother, Will, survived until 1997, when he was around eighty-four years of age.

Olive Redman nee Bridger

Olive readily admits to being a true 'Hampshire Hog', having been born at Whitehill in 1937. Her father, James Bridger, had originated from Liss and his main occupation during his working life had been as a boiler attendant at the various Army barracks – Louisburg, Martinique, Guadaloupe, Havannah etc - around Bordon Garrison. Olive's mother, also Olive by name, came from Rogate and married James in 1934 at Petersfield. Prior to her marriage, Olive senior had been the head sewing-maid at the highly regarded Bedales School at Steep. Their second daughter, Jean, now lives at Purewell, near Christchurch.

Olive's infant education was undertaken at St Matthew's Primary School, Blackmoor, in the days when that school was located in what is now Blackmoor Village Hall, adjacent to the apple-packing station. She recalls that the headmaster was Mr 'Tommy' Adlam, who had returned from military service at the end of the war, and was the proud holder of the Victoria Cross (VC). Another memory she has is of an oil painting of the then Lord Selborne, which used to hang in the main hall. Irreverently, the schoolboys of the day used to flick ink darts at the painting, to such an extent that it became almost impossible to see the portrait below the ink stains!

(Lieutenant Colonel Tom Edwin Adlam was a hero of the Battle of the Somme, which took place in France during World War I. During that battle, in 1916, the then young Lieutenant led an attack, against heavy opposition, on the German Army's fortified trenches. Despite being twice wounded, Lt Adlam's leadership inspired his men to secure their objective and infiltrate a whole enemy position. He refused to leave the battlefront for the next two days, until ordered to do so by his Commanding Officer. His bravery won him Britain's highest military honour. After being called up again, for service in the Second World War, Tom returned to his teaching profession at Blackmoor until retirement. He died in 1974 at the age of eighty-two. A portrait of the brave veteran now hangs in the Guildhall of his hometown of Salisbury. Ed.)

Olive and her mother used to both belong to the choir at Blackmoor Church, but after a *contretemps* with the vicar, decided to start taking the bus down to **Greatham** each Sunday. That would have been around 1954 and Olive was still a member of the **Greatham Church** choir some thirty-eight years later. No doubt this long spell of service was assisted by the fact that, when she joined, Edgar was already a member! It wasn't long before he was offering Olive a lift home after the church service and this eventually led to their wedding in February 1959. The harmony continued for many years, as Olive and Edgar would sit around the table, planning which hymns and psalms would be used for the following Sunday.

The 'daily round' proved a hard one as Olive settled down to village life here in **Greatham**. Those were the days when Edgar had a large herd of cattle, and Olive 'mucked in' as an extra pair of hands. As well as cleaning all the dairy equipment, she looked after a few chickens at one time, carried out the gardening tasks and looked after not only her husband, but also his father William and his brother, another William. There was the added burden of having to look after her own father at his Whitehill home, after her mother died in 1977. Olive used to cycle along the 'one-mile straight' between the villages, grateful for the occasions when Edgar could offer her a lift in their reliable *Hillman 'Minx'*. Her father eventually ended up at the King George Sanatorium, which had once been a 'Home for Sailors'. This was located at nearby Liphook and was where James Bridger finally died in 1983.

As well as these homely duties, Olive found the time to join in with many aspects of village life, including membership of the Women's Institute, Parish Council and Parochial Church Council. She recalls that Sunday always seemed the hardest day of all, having to get ready for Church as well as carry out the regular work of house and farm. This was especially onerous when Edgar's brother Will became ill and unable to 'do his bit'. Today, with only her son David and four cats to look after, she finds life just a pale shadow of what it once was.

St Matthew's Church, Blackmoor, where Olive sang in the choir

*David Redman
and his trusty
'John Deere' tractor*

David Redman

Olive has fond memories of David being taken for 'walks' by his grandfather, William. These would inevitably end up not too far away from the Woolmer Hotel, with David being left outside to enjoy a packet of crisps! David went to **Greatham School** and stayed on until the age of, as Olive puts it, nine and three-quarters! It had been the intention that he would then go on to Churcher's College in Petersfield, but in fact continued his education at Little Abbey Preparatory School up at Langley, Rake. (It is surely only coincidence that the school was used as the background for the shooting of one of the St Trinian's films!) He stayed on until the age of fourteen, forced to leave when the school closed due to a problem with the lease.

David then went on to attend Clark's College, where he found the most pleasure was in the daily train journeys between Liss and Guildford! He used to cycle down to Liss Station to catch the train, once almost having a nasty accident in an altercation with an Army lorry, being driven by a learner driver. Upon ending his educational life at sixteen, David found some temporary employment, potato picking at a farm between Hawkley and Wheatham. He also carried out duties as a general farm labourer, but soon decided that he would like to strike out for himself.

His mother recalls David sitting down with father Edgar, discussing which tractor ought to be purchased. The chosen one was a *'John Deere'*, which is still David's proud possession some thirty years later. Working as an agricultural contractor, David will turn his hand to just about anything he is asked to. If there is any trenching, digging, cutting down, pulling or pushing to be done in **Greatham**, you can be sure that David and his tractor will soon be in the vicinity! At present he is busily engaged on cutting the grass on the embankments that lie alongside the famous *'Watercress Line'*.

(The 'Watercress Line' is a railway line that runs between the towns of Alton and Alresford, here in Hampshire. At Alton, a link can be made with the national rail network, while the Watercress Line itself is privately owned and run by enthusiasts. It is part of the old British Railways secondary route from Alton to Winchester and Southampton, which was finally closed in 1973 despite desperate local attempts to save it. It was originally intended that the

Peter Gripton

Funeral cortege at Longmoor Camp (from the Redman collection)

whole route would be re-opened after the Mid-Hants Railway Company bought it, but events precluded this – not least of all the construction of the M3 motorway across the route.

'History in motion' can be experienced by travelling under the power of steam or on a heritage diesel train. From the busy market town of Alton, the single line to Alresford passes along ten miles of steeply graded track through beautiful Hampshire scenery via two intermediate stations, where passing points allow up-and-down journeys to run at the same time. Ropley provides the railway's engineering base, while Medstead/Four Marks is the highest station (652 feet above sea level) in southern England. The steep hills either side of Medstead gave rise to this section becoming well known as 'Over the Alps'. Alresford, on the River Arle, is of the Georgian era and it is here that the watercress beds can be seen, from which the railway took its marketing name. Ed.)

Further Wells connections

Readers of **'A History of Greatham'** will recall the section (see chapter 37) devoted to the family antecedents of the Redman family, the large Wells family, which had so many connections with **Greatham**. During the early part of 2007, Olive and David Redman came across a bundle of documents that included letters, receipts, and seed catalogues, amongst other things. There were also a few copies each of two old photographs, printed (as was the style of those days) as postcards, and showing what must be part of a military funeral procession at Longmoor Camp, presumably at some time between 1910 and 1920. I say this, because I already had a similar photograph in my own collection of **Greatham** memorabilia, inscribed with the words *'Funeral Cortege, Longmoor Camp'*.

Taking pride of place however, in this 'bundle' was a solicitor's statement from 1925, which gives us a fascinating glimpse into the extent of the Wells family in those far off days. It can also be tied in neatly with a lot of the documentation already published in my earlier book. I publish the letter verbatim on the next page.

The details were slightly 'tidied up' for presentation, while several words on the original document were rather obscure and had to be 'guessed at'. The 'Emma Jane' at 6a. was born in 1877 and married William Albert Redman in 1911. They were the parents of Edgar Redman, born in 1914, who married Olive Bridger in 1959. Their only son, David, was born later that same year.

> **Re - MATILDA CHALMERS DECEASED**
> Late of 21 CROWNDALE ROAD, CAMDEN TOWN
> DECEASED died on the 30th JANUARY 1925 intestate and LETTERS OF ADMINISTRATION of her ESTATE were GRANTED by the PRINCIPAL PROBATE REGISTRY of HIS MAJESTY'S HIGH COURT of JUSTICE on the 27th MARCH 1925 to MR GEORGE WELLS, a nephew of DECEASED.
> Deceased died a widow without issue, and without Parent or Grandparent surviving her.
> Deceased had twelve Brothers and Sisters as follows:
> 1. ANNE WELLS who died in infancy
> 2. ALFRED WELLS who died in infancy
> 3. GEORGE WELLS who died a Bachelor, without issue
> 4. LOUSIA WELLS who died a spinster, without issue
> 5. JOHN WELLS who died, leaving 5 children as follows:
> a. George Wells, Runsfold
> b. William Wells, Victory Inn, Station Road, Chertsey
> c. Ann Covey, Hoodington Arms, Upton Gray, Winchfield
> d. Caroline Charlotte Wells, 4 Draycott Place, Sloane Square, SW3
> e. Ellen Edith Gowing, 101 Bristol Road, Forest Gate, E7
> 6. JAMES WELLS who died leaving 3 children as follows:
> a. Emma Jane Redman of Rooks Farm, **Greatham**, Liss
> b. James Wells of Grigg's Green, Liphook
> c. Alfred Wells of Grayshott, Surrey
> 7. MARY SIMMONDS who died leaving 1 child viz:
> a. Alfred Simmonds, Honors Farm, Bovingdon, Hemel Hempstead
> 8. DANIEL WELLS who died leaving 3 children viz:
> a. George Wells, 301 West End Lane, Hampstead
> b. Walter Wells, 16 Cavendish Street, Shirebrook, Mansfield
> c. Daniel Wells, 34 Forbury Road, Southsea
> 9. CAROLINE MOSS who died leaving 2 children viz:
> a. Matilda Dawe, 46 Stoke Newington Road
> b. Kate Moss, 46 Stoke Newington Road
> 10. WILLIAM WELLS, living in **Greatham**, Petersfield
> 11. HARRIETT EDWIN, living at 28 Landport Terrace, Southsea
> 12. ELLEN DANCE, living at 'The Lilacs', Heathrow, Hounslow

Further revelations?

Having returned from my summer holiday in August 2007, I had a stored phone message from Pat Flack, asking me to call her back. I must confess to not doing that very quickly, but meeting up with David Redman, he told me that there was 'another branch of the (Wells) family' who had recently been in contact with himself and Olive. I then spoke with Pat to pass on my e-mail address and, shortly afterwards, I received the following e-mail:

"Pat Flack spoke to you yesterday about my visit to her and Olive Redman. By way of introduction, my name is Ray Wells and I am a direct descendant of Peter Wells of Selborne, circa 1620. I have been, with others, researching our family tree. Others include a lady I have not met, Mrs Lynn Wells (formerly of Longbeech Drive, Southwood), who compiled the tree I am sending to Olive, as well as Natalie Mees (Archivist at the Gilbert White Museum) and my niece LeeAnn Beer (who has done research for the Wells Family web-site - mostly run from the USA unfortunately). I also have various other publications, including Rupert Willoughby's book on Selborne. I am a novice, having taken up research on my retirement two years ago, but my particular interest is in expanding the family tree and using the it to gather history of the family's lives, work and movements. My branch of the Wells family moved to Portsmouth in the mid-1800s, we assume to work in the expanding Dockyard areas, as

they were blacksmiths, wheelwrights and bricklayers.

My father died in 1994, but I have two brothers (one, Richard, living in Canada from my father's first marriage) and a sister. When Richard visited the UK for the first time in July, we were shown round 'Wheelwrights' in Gracious Street, Selborne - a property that we owned (we think) from the early 1700s into the 1800s. Although I only collected your book **'A History of Greatham'** *from Pat yesterday, she purchased it on my behalf several weeks ago. I have already had a good read. The photos of Billy Wells, The Queen and the blacksmith shop (with actual Wells family members in it?) were fascinating. My Canadian relatives would find them most interesting.*

I will be returning to **Greatham** *at some stage to meet Olive again (she has so much anecdotal information on the Wells family in her head) and to meet David Redmond. Well I had better go, I have your book and another on Newton Valence to read, to broaden my knowledge on the history of the area."*

I did in fact meet up with Ray when he next visited *Greatham*, and I feel that I am almost a family member now! Ray's own research, leading on from what I had previously gleaned and what he has since scrupulously gathered together, is presented below:

Notes from Ray Wells regarding his connections in *Greatham*

GEORGE WELLS: Born 1812 in Selborne, the son of Thomas (1773 – 1851) and Martha Ansell (1783 - ?). Occupation: Wheelwright (1841), Wheelwright and Blacksmith (1851 and 1861), Wheelwright, Blacksmith and Publican (1871, 1881). He is also described as a farmer in latter years. Married Harriett (dates not known - can probably find out in due course) from Headley and had 13 children.

George appears to be the founding member of the *Greatham* branch of the Wells family. He was a Wheelwright/Blacksmith, as were his father and at least one brother in Selborne. A move to a nearby large village may therefore have been a natural progression, particularly as the roads to and from Selborne have been built around 1820/30. Prior to this road development, Selborne had been virtually cut off from neighbouring villages by deep, rutted, tree root-strewn muddy paths. Throughout his time in *Greatham*, George expanded his business and property portfolio so that, by 1889, not as result of Harriett's death (she was still going strong in 1891), the Trustees of George had a substantial holding of land and cottages up for sale. The *Queen's Head* public house, now known as *The Greatham Inn*, appears to have been sold before 1881. There is a story that says the Wells family built the pub in circa 1830 (see sign above the pub), but I have not been able to substantiate this to date.

The children:

ALFRED: (birth date not known). Died in infancy, no trace on any census return.

GEORGE jnr: (1834 - ?). Also a Wheelwright, he married Jane Janes (dates not known) although possibly Janes was her surname. They have no children recorded on census returns. The 1861 census shows they were living at Todmore Cottages but by 1881 and through to 1901, had moved to Stedham, where George is working as a Wheelwright and Blacksmith. In 1881, they have a Martin Kemp (a well-known Selborne family name and his birthplace), aged 15, lodging as a trainee Blacksmith. In 1901, aged in their mid-60s, George and Jane have the Billard family with them, working as Agricultural Machinery repairers. The address then was The Alley, Stedham.

JAMES: (1836 - ?). A Blacksmith, he firstly appears as married to Ann (dates not known - but can probably find out), born 1852 in Newton Valence. No known children. He then married Harriett (surname not known - check where born and trace? (1839 -1883)). They had children Alfred (1866), James (1869), Martin (1871-1897) and Emma Jane (1877). Martin died in Emsworth, following some kind of accident. James jnr (1869) appears to have moved to Bramshott to work as a Blacksmith and then to have married Frances M Moss (b.1868 in Chichester), the daughter of Benjamin and Clara Moss from Bramshott. Benjamin Moss's second wife was Caroline Wells (1851), daughter of George (1812) and Harriett. The Moss family was large and well-known in Bramshott. Emma Jane (xxxx) married William Redman (xxxx-xxxx) from Blackmoor and had a son Edgar. Edgar married Olive xxxx in 1959 and they have a son, **DAVID REDMAN**.

JOHN: (1838). In 1861 census, he is shown as a Wheelwright lodging with Thomas Smith, also a Wheelwright, of Bramley. No further clear trace of John in census returns, but 'possible' John Wells shown as a shepherd, born in Bradfield with wife (xxxx) and children (see 1871 census print out). However, children living (known from 1925 probate document) as Charlotte Caroline, Ann, William, Ellen Edith, George and William. Names similar to 1871 children listed but John shown as born 1832, but link tenuous. We do know, from probate document, Ann married

xxxxxx Covey and Ellen E married xxxxxx Gowan, but to date no trace found via census returns.

MARY JANE: (1840). In 1861 was working as a cook servant at home of Sparkes family in Wonersh. Hereafter I had problems, until I discovered that her married name was SIMMONS, not Simmonds as shown in the probate document of 1925. In 1871, Mary is married to William Simmons, a farmer's servant, aged 44 born and living in Bovingdon, Herts. By 1881, Alfred, their son, is aged 9 and William is a Wood and Coal Merchant on own account. Similar in 1891, but Alfred not at home and not traced to date. In 1901, no sign of William or Mary, but Alfred has married Beatrice (not known), born 1873 in Broomfield, Essex and they have a daughter Dorothy, born 1897. In addition, they have a groom/servant lodging and live in Luck's Lane, Bovingdon.

LOUISA: (1843). Appears to have remained single all her life and is shown living with parents and then, in 1861, at Forest Side and *Queen's Head* public house as landlady in 1871/81. To date, no trace in 1891 or 1901. Date of death not known, but she was dead at time of 1925 probate document.

ANN: (1844-1855).

DANIEL: (1847-1879). Was married to Louisa (not known), born 1853 in Southampton. Children: George (1874), Walter A (1877) and Daniel jnr (1879) - the same year as his father died. In 1871, Daniel is living with parents and working as a Coach-builder but by 1881 he is deceased and his widow Louisa (single name not known) is Postmistress and living at Todmore Cottages. In 1891 still postmistress, but living at New Cottage, Main Street but she has vanished from census reports by 1901.

DANIEL jnr: (the son, 1879) is listed as a Seaman in 1901, 'living' in Southsea but there is no further news of him, save he does not seem to appear amongst the 1914-18 war dead in **Greatham**. Walter A (1877) is shown in 1891 census as a servant in Croydon, at what appears to be the Hydropathic Hotel. In 1901, no specific trace, but there is a Wells from Alton born 1877 on board *'HMS Kestrel'* in Birkenhead. It is not possible to identify as Walter A. George, a servant at home of Bickers family in Colwall, Herefordshire in 1891, but married to Constance Lindfield (born 1881 in Handcross), with a son born 1901. George is working as a Hairdresser in Station Road and has a lodger, and Esther Lindfield (mother-in-law) visiting.

HARRIETT: (1848). Married to Nicholas Edwin (b 1849 in **Greatham**), who was a Coach Painter. Children: twins Alice M (1879) and Ellen M (1879), George N (1882), Edith H (1884) and Rosa A (1883). In 1871, Harriett is a servant at home of George and Mary Ann Thorn in Landport Terrace, Southsea, but by 1881 and same for further census reports, is married and living at 28 Landport Terrace,

Southsea. Nicholas was at home address in 1871, but appears to have a wife, Carlina Edwin (born 1879 in Dublin) at Mitchell's Yard, Portsea. No further trace of Carlina

11

after 1871.

CAROLINE: (1852). In 1871 census, Caroline is living at home in **Greatham**. Benjamin Moss (her future husband it would seem) is aged 33 (1838), an Edge Tool Maker and married to Clara (nee Harding). She is 32 (1839) and was born in Frensham. They had two children, Clara (1866) and Frances (1868), mentioned here, as one becomes significant to the Wells family. Both were born in Southgate, Chichester, Sussex and there was a lodger, Mary A Durman, acting as a servant, aged 16 and from Privett. By 1881, Caroline is married to Benjamin Moss and living at Woolmer Forest, Bramshott with Frances M Moss. By 1891, there are children Matilda (1884) and Kate or Caroline (?) born 1886 with Caroline (1852) listed as a Grocer but at Deer's Hut, Bramshott. There is no trace of Clara in 1881/91 searches so far.

I have some census printouts that show the Moss family to be a large and important family in Bramshott. In 1901, Matilda is boarding at what looks like a school address, 2 Wishingwell Place, Stoke Within, Guildford. Frances M Moss is aged 34 and married to James Wells, born 1869 in **Greatham** - the son of Caroline's brother James (1836) and is a Blacksmith in Bramshott. There is one child, also James Wells (1900). Address given as 'near' Deer's Hut, Bramshott.

Note - Clara Moss (nee Harding) born 1839/40 in Frensham and has a brother

James Harding (1838), who in 1861 was a visiting Wheelwright at home of Amy

King, widow and owner of Abinger's Wheelwright. William King, son of Amy, was also listed as a Wheelwright.

WILLIAM (1855). Lived in **Greatham** all his life and was well known as 'Billy' Wells. He was a Carpenter and Wheelwright. At the age of 35 (1891 census), he was living with his mother Harriett at New Cottage, Main Street or Rose Cottage (some confusion). In 1901, shown as married to Mary Wakeford (1850), born in Rogate. Mary was single in 1891 and cook/domestic servant to Constance Smith (1819 aged 72) at the Smith's home, address given as 'Private House', **Greatham**. There is a sale notice, undated, in Peter's book for a Lees Cottage, which refers to 'the late Mrs Wells' (this could refer to Billy's mother) and states 'currently occupied by William Wells'. William had no children.

ELLEN: (1858), one of twins. Ellen married John Charles Dance, but in 1881 census is shown as visitor to Louisa, widow of Daniel, at Todmore Cottages. Ellen is described as a Coachman's wife and John Charles is listed at 24 Brook Mews North, Paddington, as a lodger and Coachman. In 1891, John is a Bean Retailer (?) living at George Green, Eton, with Ellen and two children, Clara Ellen (1882, born **Greatham**), Edith (1886), Alice (1888) and Millicent (1889), all born in Langley, Berks. By 1901, listed as Market Gardeners (under name Douce – census mistake), address High Street, Harmonsworth. At the time of the 1925 probate, Ellen is living at The Lilacs, Heathrow, Hounslow. 1901 no trace of Clara but Alice and Millicent at home with parents and Edith (under Dance) is a servant at Sion House, Sion Road, Twickenham, the home of Frederick (1864) and William Chapman (1834), son and father.

Note - Sion House, Twickenham has been the London home of the Duke of Northumberland since the 1500s.

MATILDA: (1858). Married to John Chalmers (1858), a house painter born in Berwickshire. At home in 1871, by 1881 a servant to Elliott family at 5 Manor Road, Lewisham. (Matilda is spelt Matlida Wells in census.) 1891 married and living at 14 Pancras Street, St. Pancras, London. John described as a decorator in 1891 and 1901 but, by the latter, had moved to 23 Tottenham Street, St. Pancras. There are no children. It is Matilda's probate document, dated 1925, (found by Olive and David Redman), which gives the most clues to tracing the **Greatham** branch of the Wells family line.

Footnote - Nothing found so far in the **Greatham** branch of the family to suggest that there is a link to Herbert George (H G) Wells, famous author of *'War of the Worlds'*.

Chapter 3
Julia Fisher nee Coryton

There may well be just a few **Greatham** villagers who still remember Julia Coryton, as she then was, now living as Mrs Julia Fisher down near Cirencester in Gloucestershire. During the writing of my reference book *'A History of Greatham'*, I was delighted to make her acquaintance, along with her husband Richard, when they visited the village in the summer of 2003. Meeting at Goulds House, thanks to the hospitality of Anna Dale-Harris, the couple was able to provide me with some updated facts about the Coryton family, which I was then able to include in the book. Since then, I have been able to provide Julia with several copies of the book for other members of her family. Julia has recently written to me with the following kind words:

"I have not been able to put down your book, it is all so fascinating. It is extraordinary to think that there are so very many terribly old buildings in what is not really a very pretty village. But if one stops to look into it, each individual house has such a history of its own. Many of the things you write about were just taken for granted by us when living there seventy years ago. How times have changed! You really have given the neighbourhood a beautifully put together 'memento'. My copy will be very precious."

Along with her letter (and another book order!), Julia also included a copy of the funeral address that was given for her father, Augustus Coryton, by one Michael Lee QC back in March 1976. It is written in longhand and I have yet to decipher every word but, when I have managed to do that, I

Coryton family members at Manor House in 1907

will publish it in a future article for all to read. It makes a wonderful tribute to the man who has often been described as **'The last Squire of Greatham'**.

I responded as follows:

"Thank you for your letter Julia, wonderful to hear from you once again. I am pleased that the book has continued to be so well received around the village and am proud that it has also reached such far-off places as Australia, France, Iceland and Northern Ireland. I had the pleasure of bumping into Andy Mitchell just a few days ago. I can't remember meeting him before and he now lives in France, where he runs his own guitar school near Toulouse. He was so pleased to have read the book, belonging to his mother, that he was going to take it back to France with him, so that he can show 'the locals' over there just where he used to live."

The Coryton family name

A small village in the county of Devon, just to the west of Dartmoor, still bears the name of Coryton and it is from this place that the **Greatham** branch of the family originated. The name is taken from the Celtic Saint Curig, who lived in the county in the early 6th century. The Saxon missal of Leofric names it as Curigtown and it is not difficult to see how this later became corrupted into 'Coryton'. After the Norman Conquest, in 1086, the manor of Coryton was given to a family from Normandy, who then took the name 'de Corytone'. The Corytons moved to Pentillie Castle in Cornwall around 1600 and are commemorated by several monuments in the nearby church at St Mellion.

Chapter 4
Captain Coryton

As a follow-up to an article that I wrote regarding the Coryton family, I am now able to publish the contents of the address that was presented at Augustus Coryton's funeral service. Some of the content may be slightly different from the original, as I was working from a hand-written script, with nobody now to refer to. But I am sure that what follows is as accurate as can be and presents an insight into the life led by Captain Coryton over a great portion of the twentieth century.

Address in Greatham Church, March 5th 1976

"We are gathered here today, in the church of which he was Churchwarden and read the lesson for many years, to say *"Goodbye and God be with you"* to Augustus Frederick Coryton. His has been a long life, for he was born in 1892 and, therefore, this is not an occasion for sadness but rather for reflection upon the pleasure of the character and achievements of this nice man.

August Frederick Coryton JP, last 'Lord of the Manor'

He came, along with his father in 1899, from Lyss Place to the Manor House in this village. He went to Harrow School and then to Magdalene College, Cambridge, and so, when he was twenty-one in 1913, that 'golden year', he could have expected to lead a useful and uninterrupted life looking after the welfare of the village as Lord of the Manor.

All was changed however in the next year, 1914. Let no one of a later generation ever forget what he and his young companions had to undergo in 'The Great War'. To the filth and degradation of the Flanders trenches they went, again and again, with undiminished courage. It is surely the fact that those young men, who enlisted as the King's professional Army met its death at Mons, were the finest body of men that ever went into battle, in defence of this country. Alas, the flower of the nation's youth was all but destroyed and those who miraculously survived were gravely wounded in body and spirit by the almost intolerable conditions.

Captain Coryton served throughout the whole war in the 14/18th Hussars, in France and Flanders. He hardly ever spoke of those years afterwards, for he was the most modest of men. But we know that he showed high courage and was greatly loved by the men under his command. He was badly gassed on one occasion and was later buried alive by the mud thrown up by a shell-burst. It is not surprising that his health was gravely impaired by the year 1918. I say again, let no one forget what this Captain did, or squander the prize of freedom that he and his brothers-in-arms won by their fortitude.

After some years of convalescence, he resumed his life here in **Greatham** and, for over forty years, patiently worked his land and gently helped all the people of the village, both young and old, who needed assistance. This was the basis of his life and his was a good life. He also performed many public duties, too numerous to mention. He was a man of great courtesy, I never heard him speak ill of any man.

I first met him in the middle Twenties, when he came to dinner with my family. We were a young, large and noisy family, but I remember to this day the courtesy with which he drew back the chair at the table for my youngest sister, then insisted on calling her '*Ma'am*' and behaving most charmingly. That very evening, I acquired a deep respect for him that I never lost and, I must shyly add, I also acquired a new respect for my youngest sister.

Let us now turn to his other activities. In the winter months, he had an abiding love of hunting. He was the Honorary Secretary of the Hampshire Hunt from 1920 to 1933, and then again from 1948 to 1963. Lots of words are spoken, many of them uninformed, about hunting. But surely he is a dull-spirited fellow who does not feel his heart rise at the sight of the Hunt, moving off to the first covert? Long will the Hampshire Hunt survive, so long as it has the support of champions such as he.

Augustus loved cricket at all levels – village cricket, club cricket for the 'Hampshire Hogs' and county cricket. Perhaps he loved village cricket best, for something pretty odd was bound to happen during any match on the village green. Many were the games he captained on the field behind the Manor House. He was a very good captain, self-effacing as always, keen to give everyone a chance to show promise, and ready to applaud any good performance, whether by friend or foe. I remember his bat, the blade of which, by repeated application of linseed oil, had acquired a rich mahogany colour and which gave out a deep sound, worthy of a Stradivarius violin, whenever it drove a ball to the boundary.

He took a great interest in the feats of the County cricket side in the days before the Second World War. Those were the days of that great pair of bowlers, Newman and Kennedy, of that astute and elephantine figure, Phil Mead, and of that most adventurous captain, Lionel Tennyson. Augustus was the Vice-President of the County Club to the day of his death and took great pleasure in the successes of the present side under Richard Gilliatt and Barry Richards. His enthusiasm for the game gained many new supporters for the Club.

From 1928, until his retirement in 1962 on reaching the ripe old age of seventy, he was a Justice of the Peace, presiding on the local Petersfield bench, and always a figure of strength. I remember arguing a case before that bench, thirty years ago, on behalf of some alleged malefactors. I gained comfort from his presence next to the Chairman, for he was patient and wise. As the magistrates filed out to consider their verdict, I thought I saw, maybe I was mistaken, the tiniest but reassuring wink from Justice Coryton, as he passed me by. I do not recall the result of the case, only that justice was done.

In 1956, he became High Sherriff and, again, I remember his dignified and reassuring presence, even next to the Judge of Assize, in the ancient court at Winchester. For, in those days, Judges needed constant attention and Sherriff Coryton looked well after their needs. In 1958 he was made a Deputy Lieutenant for the County, an honour that he richly deserved, for he was a dedicated Hampshireman.

But his great and abiding joy stemmed first from his marriage, in 1931, to Miss Violet Shuttleworth, then from his three daughters and his grandchildren. Augustus always had a great love of children and they turned instinctively towards him, while he was always most kind and understanding to them. Four years ago, he and his wife moved from the Manor House to the smaller Goleigh farmhouse nearby and so then, I suppose, an era came to an end. But the village community had been closely knit together by his care over the years and I have no doubt that the men and women of *Greatham* will continue to care for each other, as he would wish.

And so, in our memories will remain his high qualities, his courage, his love of children and his sense of fun; but perhaps best of all, his abiding courtesy. To Mrs Coryton, to Violet, from all of us goes our sincere sympathy. But perhaps she may find a little solace in this, that we will ever remember how together, she and her gentle husband gave great pleasure, by their great kindness, to many people over many years. We thank both her and our dear friend, Augustus Frederick Coryton."

Michael Lee QC
(Edited by Peter Gripton, February 2004)

Peter Gripton

Chapter 5
Deal Farm

Deal Farm lies to the north west of *Greatham's* 'village street', which used to form part of the main A325 road between Petersfield to the south and Farnham to the north. It is set back from and parallel to that road, in a prominent position where the ground rises towards the village school. An earlier drover's way would have passed to the south west of the building, as indicated on early maps of the area. The house itself is remarkably unchanged, mainly because its original form has adapted so easily to modern living, and it dates back to the second or third quarter of the 17th century i.e. 1650 - 1700. Externally, however, there have been many changes over the years and, at one stage, a large wooden barn bore the name of 'Henry Trigg', who appears to have run the farm on behalf of Viscount Wolmer.

Sue and Alan Booton moved into their Deal Farm home in October 2002. Their daughter, Wendy McCann, was already a teacher at the local school here, commuting on a daily basis from her home in Wrecclesham. Alan's father had been involved in the building supplies business and, although Alan's own background had been in the engineering trade, over the years he had also developed a keen interest in the conservation and restoration of old buildings. No doubt this interest had been sparked during his younger days, when he would wander around the site of Waverley Abbey near Farnham, the first ever Cistercian Abbey to be built in England.

(The Abbey was founded by the then Bishop of Winchester, William Giffard, on Christmas Day in the year 1128. The monks, of whom there were just twelve, arrived with their Abbot from the Convent of D'Aumone, in Normandy. This itself was an offshoot of the great Cistercian Abbey of Cisteaux, from where the order derived its name. The founder of the order was a man named Harding, born in England of simple working-class parents, and who had originally been a monk at Sherbourne, in Dorset. He had grown tired of his monastic life and went first to Scotland and afterwards to France, where he again became awakened by the love of God. Proceeding to Rome, he continued his studies and, on returning to France, he later founded the great Cistercian order. The last Abbot of Waverley,

The Trigg/Gilbert wedding party at Deal Farm, 1907

18

William Ayling, surrendered the estate into the hands of local Commissioners in 1536. This part of the dissolution of the monasteries, engendered under King Henry VIII and Thomas Cromwell. On the fate of the Abbot and monks of Waverley, history has stayed silent. But it certain that they were turned out, homeless and penniless, into the wide world, with their goods and belongings handed over to royal favourites.

I am indebted for this information on the Abbey, contained in a book in Alan's possession, written by Rev Charles Kerry in 1872. Ed.)

The Booton name

Although he has no documentary evidence of a family connection, Alan has been fascinated to find that his unusual surname is the same as that of a small hamlet in Norfolk, located some ten miles north of Norwich. That village, Booton, is mentioned in the Domesday Book in reference to the county, then known as 'Norfulc', while there is also the splendid Booton Hall nearby. This is a Grade II 18th-century listed country house with Tudor origins, built in the grounds of the earlier 17th-century Booton Manor. One of these days, Alan swears that he will get around to trying to trace back his roots, hoping to find a link back to some possible Norfolk antecedents. *(Having said that, Alan also has connections with the north-east, having originated from Stockton-on-Tees, while he also knows that there is a large Booton contingent in Daventry, Nothants!)*

Having previously lived in the Farnham area for many years, when Deal Farm came onto the market, he knew it was 'just the place' for him. To be frank, some of the 'improvements' that had been carried out in previous years did not meet the 'Booton seal of approval'. Thus, for the past eighteen months, Alan has spent a lot of time and effort in trying to restore the farmhouse to something like its original condition, while Sue is now endeavouring to bring back a bit of life and colour into the gardening side of things.

When he read the fascinating story by Ronald (or Ron) Shotter in the book *'A History of Greatham'*, Alan got in touch with Ron at his home in south London. Since then, they have maintained contact and Ron has been able to provide many details of just how Deal Farm was laid out during the nineteen-fifties. Alan has himself been able to find traces of old sheds, barns, water troughs and the like, although the septic tank sewage system is one thing he wishes had been removed and replaced! At the time of writing, he has harnessed the power of David Redman and his tractor to try and sort out a flooding problem.

Alan has been both surprised and obviously delighted by the number of artefacts and strange objects that he has found either hidden or just discarded both in and around the house. Chief object of interest must be the small child's shoe that he found tucked away on a ledge inside one of the chimney breasts. Probably dating back to around the time that the house was first built, he has been told that the placement of such an object would have been looked upon as a 'good luck charm' and that the shoe should now always remain inside Deal Farm. Other objects, which may or not be man-made, he found in the earth and streams

Deal Fram today, home to Sue and Alan Booton

19

around the property, and he has promised to take to a local museum sometime, in order to get an expert opinion.

Early days

Alan has been able to obtain a copy of an old map, showing the layout of the area around the farm when it was actually under the jurisdiction of two separate farms, known as *'Deal Nap Farm'* and *'Tanner's Farm'*. It is unfortunate that the map is torn across, just to the north of Deal Nap, but there is sufficient to show the area just across the road, then literally *'Baker's Field'*. A well-used footpath or 'green lane' then ran from just south of Deal Nap, to then cross what is now Church Lane and continue as far as the Hawkley Road. The map pre-dates the building of the 'new' church in 1875, and the strip of land that runs parallel to and to the north of what is now Church Lane was then known as *'Shepherd's Mead'*.

An accompanying document indicates the lands that belonged to the two named farms as follows:

The gold sovereign

In the middle of 2006, Alan phoned me to say that he had a curious tale to tell! As previously mentioned, Alan has kept closely in touch with Ron Shotter, who has been instrumental in telling Alan just how the farm used to be laid out in earlier years. This has allowed Alan to restore the farm back to much of its former layout, both the interior and outlying areas. Alan once asked Ron, *"Who had the farm before your family?"* To which Ron answered *"Old farmer Adams"*. He also went on to say that Mr Adams had constantly re-visited the farm, just after the Shotter family had moved in, asking whether anyone had found the gold sovereign he had lost.

Alan became fascinated by this tale of a lost coin, which had apparently been lost 'somewhere along the drive'. He knew that the old entrance to the farm, and any associated drive, was located much differently to the present day. Enlisting the assistance of a local archaeological group, along with metal detectors, Alan began to search for the missing sovereign. Various metal artefacts turned up, in the shape of old coins, buttons and badges, including a musket ball, a small cattle bell and a loom weight. The latter item would date back to Tudor times, when people in isolated communities would use spinning devices to make their own yarn and clothing.

Alan then received a call from Ron Shotter, who told him that 'old farmer Adams' was in fact 'old farmer Trigg'! This name certainly tied in with other received information, and it then transpired that the gold sovereign had been lost on the day of the wedding-party photograph taken outside Deal Farm in 1907. Alan called in the metal detector man, James Foster, who then hinted that he had a theory of his own! Checking against old drawings of the farm layout, James began to search again and, to his delight and amazement, found the missing coin! It was in virtually the same condition as the day it had been lost, a 1907 Edward VII gold sovereign, which certainly illustrates the endurability of that precious metal.

It would be far more believable if that sovereign

Land belonging to Deal Nap Farm and Tanner's Farm

Deal Nap Farm	***Tanner's Farm***
Wreathen Wood Field	*The Garden Yard*
Kinchet's Field	*The Platt*
Mead Field	*Bakers Field*
Moor Croft	*The Five acres*
The Garden and Yards	*Shepherd's Innermost Mead*
The Eight Acres	*Shepherd's Middle Mead*
Pryor's Croft	*Shepherd's Outermost Mead*
Church Field	*Five Acres Pasture Piece*
Long Croft	
Wreathen Mead	
The Alder Moor	
Bridge Mead	
Long Croft Pasture	

had been found purely by chance! The fact that it had been lost and that someone then deliberately set out to locate it - and actually found it on a site measuring some four acres – is definitely a tale worth telling. Alan invited me around to Deal Farm to see the coin, and was able to show me the amazing collection of items that have turned up from beneath the ground since he arrived in Greatham just three-and-a-half years previously. One item of green-glazed pottery took my eye. Sadly it is now only a small shard of what must have been a handsome Tudor jug in its day, with the shape of a face arranged as the jug's spout. Alan also has collected a great amount of correspondence concerning Deal Farm and is obviously deeply interested in the whole history of what is now his splendid home.

Footnote

Just prior to publication of *'A History of Greatham'*, Ron Shotter had come across a very poignant 'funeral card' and photograph, which he had discovered in the belongings of his Aunt Emily, who had once temporarily lived at Rook's Farm, before settling at Deal Farm. He very kindly thought that this item should reside in **Greatham** and thus I was privileged to become its proud owner. The photograph shows Frederick Charles Hiscock, a young Trooper with the 19th and 11th Hussars, and son of Charles and Louisa Mary Hiscock. Charles Hiscock was Headmaster at **Greatham School** at the time of the First World War. Sadly, Frederick had died just short of his twentieth birthday, at 24 General Hospital, Etaples, in France during 1918, from a wound received on Good Friday of that year. Emily had been born here in **Greatham**, at one of the original three Swain's Cottages in 1903, so would have been aged just fifteen when Frederick Hiscock died.

Emily never married, so Ronald has often wondered whether or not there had been some affection between his Aunt and the young soldier, whose life was to be tragically cut short. The funeral card goes on to quote the following lines:

*Trooper Hiscock son of **Greatham** School's headmaster, died 30 March 1918.*

*"On that happy Easter morning
All the graves their dead restore;
Father, sister, child and mother
Meet once more.*

*To that brightest of all meetings
Bring us, JESU CHRIST at last;
By Thy Cross, through death and judgement,
Holding fast.*
Amen."

I have to admit that I found this possibility, of a childhood romance between the young soldier and the young girl from the same village, most touching. How sad that Frederick died so close to the end of that terrible War, so that we shall probably never know the truth behind Emily's possession of that funeral card right up until her death.

Chapter 6
Lady Anne Brewis MBE 1911-2002

Although Lady Anne would be officially classed as living in Blackmoor, her cottage at the far end of Benham's Lane can no doubt properly be claimed as part of **Greatham** too! *(I would certainly like to claim Lady Anne as one of **Greatham's** inhabitants, thanks to the kindliness she showed to me when I was researching my book in regard to the story of Joe Leggett. Ed.)* Her death on March 31st 2002 brought to a close ninety-one years of active service to the community, commemorated by the worthy award of the MBE in 1998 for her tireless work in the field of nature conservation.

Lady Anne was born Anne Beatrice Mary Palmer on March 26th 1911. This was just three months after her father, Viscount Wolmer, had been elected as the Conservative and Unionist MP for the constituency of Newton-le-Willows, in Lancashire. Her growing up was divided between London and her grandfather's estate at Blackmoor. Here, she was able to roam at will, among the hills and hangers so lovingly described by the Rev Gilbert White, in his classic study, *"The Natural History of Selborne"*. It was almost as though she was destined to continue the type of work started by White towards the latter end of the 18th-century.

Like White, she was particularly interested in the region's heathland and bogs. The Army had drained many of the latter at the start of the 20th-century, only

Lady Anne, who lived out her final days at Benham's House, at the bottom of Benham's Lane

to return them to their former state in much later years. Lady Anne was an adviser to the conservation committee of the Ministry of Defence (MoD), which met regularly to discuss the use of local military land and how training might compromise the flora and fauna in the vicinity. She always ensured that great care was taken when new projects were being planned.

She married the Rev John Salisbury Brewis in 1935 and devoted many years to her husband's academic and parish work in such places as Durham and Doncaster, where he became Archdeacon. During the Second World War she taught science to students at Durham University while her father, the 3rd Earl of Selborne from 1942, served as Minister of Economic Warfare, responsible among other things for the setting up of the Special Operations Executive.

The couple moved back south in 1954 then finally to a primitive cottage on an especially idyllic corner of her nephew's estate at Blackmoor. Following her husband's death in 1972, Lady Anne was, at last, able to indulge her great passion for botany. She found great solace and stimulation in joint writing of that much acclaimed book 'The Flora of Hampshire', first published in 1996. During her long widowhood, she worked ceaselessly on behalf of the Botanical Society of the British Isles and, more parochially, as a warden for the Hampshire and Isle of Wight Trust's reserve at Noar Hill.

Lady Anne also enjoyed putting her remarkable memory at the service of all those who made their way down the treacherous – to motor vehicles! – country track that forms the furthest reaches of Benham's Lane. Family members, friends and researchers would be warmly greeted, later departing Benham's House in the sure knowledge that they had been in the presence of a real lady.

(I am grateful to Olive Redman, who provided a copy of 'The Times' obituary on Lady Anne, on which much of the above article is based. Olive recalls looking after Lady Anne's eldest daughter for three weeks in 1949, during her summer holiday from Art School. Ed.)

Peter Gripton

Chapter 7
The Old Chapel, Longmoor Road

Early in 2005, I received an e-mail from a Michael Ford and was greatly pleased to later send him a copy of my book, *'A History of Greatham'*. Michael confessed a genealogical interest in the area, in that one of his ancestors had once farmed Forestside Farm, then in Blackmoor but now firmly in **Greatham**, and presently owned by Olive Redman and her son David. *(See article on Forestside Farm. Ed.)* But Michael's main interest lies in the history of old churches and chapels in Hampshire, to which purpose he is currently carrying out research.

Having received a copy of my book, Michael later wrote to me as follows:

"I am really enjoying your book and what a nice publication it is. The dates you give for the two churches at Longmoor Camp, along with their origins, are most useful. I have been trying to locate the Methodist Chapel in the village and what a surprise that you live in the house that replaced it. And what a bit of luck, finding the old postcard.

(A copy of that postcard, found at the Maltings Market in Farnham, appeared in the history book. Ed.)

I have a date of 1887 for its erection, firstly for the Petersfield Wesleyan circuit. Then, in 1900, it became a North Hampshire Wesleyan Mission Chapel, followed by coming under the umbrella of the Petersfield and Haslemere Wesleyan circuit from 1917 onwards. The Hampshire Records Office has baptismal records from 1906 to 1963."

Wesleyan Chapel Longmoor Road, 1887 – 1963

I was delighted to receive the above information regarding the old chapel, as I had previously had little to no success when trying to find out some details via the Methodist Church governing body. Having lived in Chapel House since 1967, I now feel more strongly associated with the past, when the site on where I write this note was indeed 'hallowed ground'. My memory was also drawn back to when I was constructing a patio at the back of the house, probably some twenty or so years previously. I was clearing the ground just to the rear of the original 'french window' when I came across what looked like the edge of a marble slab of sorts. Needless to say, I didn't investigate any further, quite happy to 'let sleeping dogs lie', if that is the correct phrase to use in this context!

Chapter 8
Paul Duffet remembers

Before Paul Duffett arrived in **Greatham** to take up his ministry at St John the Baptist, the Diocese of Portsmouth had somehow failed to find where the then Patron lived or even who he/she was! Soon after Paul and his wife Anita had moved into the village, around 1980, they had a visit from a priest, who had been the Vicar of the church in the neighbouring town to them at their previous home in South Africa. That priest was sitting in their lounge in the Rectory when, to the Duffetts' great surprise, he remarked, *"I have seen that church before"*. He was referring to a painting of **Greatham Church**, hanging on one of the Rectory's walls. After racking his brain for a while, he added, *"I'm sure it was once in the room of an elderly lady to whom I took communion. Her name was Miss Luttrell-West"*!

Now by that time, Paul already knew that a Cecil Francis Luttrell-West had been Vicar of **Greatham** for many years in the thirties and had bought the 'Advowson' in order to become Patron. So he made a quick phone-call to a mutual friend in South Africa, asking him to find out if there was a connection! The friend phoned back a week later to say that he had visited the lady in question and, yes indeed, she was the great niece of the late Vicar and had herself been Patron for many years. But she had since passed this on to her nephew, who was now a farmer in the Transvaal! Paul has since forgotten that gentleman's name, but he did write to him at the time. Paul later received quite a lot of relevant material, which he says must still be in one of the church files. If Paul remembers it correctly, this good man had also sent money to John Russell, in order to refurbish the Rectory drive, sometime during the seventies.

(With Paul now living in Cambridgeshire, I took it upon myself to track down the letter mentioned above – and found that the writer's name was Peter Dinkelmann. I reproduce the gist of that letter, written on January 25th 1981, as a matter of historical reference. Ed.)

Peter Dinkelmann's letter

"When Cecil Francis (CF) Luttrell-West died, my uncle (Pat Luttrell-West, of Newcastle) was in the Merchant Navy. As my grandfather, Watson Samuel (WS) Luttrell-West was the major beneficiary of CF's will, Pat, on his next visit to England, collected the personal effects (such as the family silver) and some papers belonging to CF, which were of interest to the family. Upon CF's death, the Advowson had passed to my grandfather (WS) and, when he died in 1938, it went to my grandmother.

The family kept the papers and, when my Uncle Pat died, his widow Audrey gave them on to my mother (her sister). My mother, in turn, passed them on to me a few years later when my father died and she moved into a flat. To my chagrin, I never studied them until I received your letter. They mostly cover the genealogy of the family, which can be directly traced back, through the Sempriere family of Jersey, to the Scandinavian, Everard de Sempriere, who was born in about AD 970."

The letter continues with some personal references, but then indicates that CF Luttrell-West had himself researched some of the history of the village, producing a hand-written exercise book entitled *'History*

Greatham's St John the Baptist Church, where Paul Duffet ministered from 1980 - 1988

*of **Greatham**, Hants, AD 1900'*. Briefly, CF had attempted to trace the history of 'the living', with references to Joseph Foster (Curate in charge) 1866 – 75 and the Rev Thomas Agar Holland (Patron) 1839. CF's own father had purchased 'The Advowson of **Greatham** .... and certain lands held therewith' for the sum of £2,200 on May 25th 1891. Upon that gentleman's death, it was then passed on to his widow, who conveyed it by Deed of Gift to CF Luttrell-West on January 4th 1896.

At that time, **Greatham Parish** fell within the Diocese of Winchester and the Lord Bishop indicated that he would be reluctant for CF to present himself as Rector until he *"had been in Holy Orders for at least three years"*. CF was finally inducted on October 16th 1902. Unfortunately, the exercise book ended at that stage and no further volume has been subsequently found. Peter's letter then continues as below:

"As far as I am aware, the Title Deeds never came to South Africa and I suspect that the material part, such as any land, passed to the Church. I am also not certain as to the status of the Advowson. It passed from my grandmother to my Uncle Pat but, as far as I know, he made no specific provision for it in his will, under which the sole heir was his ex-wife Audrey, whom he had divorced some years previously.

*My grandmother did indeed pay for the tarmacadamising of the area outside of the Rectory. When my wife Tricia and I visited **Greatham** in December 1974, Rev John Russell was adamant that we see it and we had sherry with his family and some parishioners after the 11 a.m. mass. We do plan to return sometime in the next few years and will take you up on your kind offer to stay a day or so."*

The power of prayer?

Many years afterwards, when Paul had then retired to the village of Barton, in Cambridgeshire, he was asked to take a service in one of the nearby villages, Dry Drayton. One can imagine his surprise when he found out that the 'east window' was dedicated to a Rev Smith, who had

*James Lacey was the Sexton at **Greatham Church** from 1906 to 1940*

retired to **Greatham Moor**. The same gentleman had also been a Fellow of one of the Cambridge colleges. The connection recalled by Paul Duffett was that, in 1982, the church here in **Greatham** had become very low in funds, in fact at the time it was £1,800 'in the red'! Everybody naturally felt pretty depressed about that until, one day, an envelope fortuitously fell onto the doormat, containing a letter and a most welcome cheque for £2,000 from a Miss Smith!

It later transpired that she was a niece of the former Vicar and now in her ninety-third year. Paul recalls going over to her home somewhere near Midhurst, in order to thank her personally. She had explained (in her letter) that she had wanted **Greatham** to have the benefit of the gift then, rather than after she had died. Paul never discovered whether someone had tipped her off about the church's predicament or whether it was simply an answer to the congregation's prayers!

But, certainly, the church never looked back after that. *(The age of the Miss Smith in question would indicate that her uncle was the Rev William Smith, who is shown as residing at **Greatham Moor** at least between the years 1875 and 1885. Ed.)*

Postscript: Older inhabitants of Greatham may be interested to know that Paul Duffett entered the 'world of authorship' in 2007, with his book *'Collared by God'* (the reminiscences of an ordinary Parson).

Chapter 9
Jane Rolling nee Coombes

Jane Coombes, who was born in February 1956, lived in **Greatham** during all of her formative years, along with her parents Gilbert and Betty, and a younger brother, David, who entered the world in September 1959. The family originally lived in one of the row of 'Deal Cottages' and later at King's Holt Cottage, the house on the raised embankment just opposite Kingshott Cottages, on the Petersfield Road. Betty Coombes's maiden name indicates that she was a member of the Trigg family, which had been well established in Greatham for many years. *(Alan Siney's research showed a Thomas Trigg on the 1840 tithe assessment, while a Henry Trigg was shown as a farmer and later a haulage contractor, from around 1885 until well into the 1930s. Ed.)*

In May 1973, Jane was most unfortunate to meet with a horrific accident, at the age of seventeen. On her way home from Highbury Technical College in Portsmouth, she was knocked down by a motorcycle, which was being ridden by a marine engineer. He had just completed his training course and had been celebrating – a little too much – with his fellow students. Poor Jane was the only one hurt and she lay unconscious for many months at hospitals in the city of Portsmouth. Although unaware of it at the time, Jane later found out that a tremendous amount of help, by friends and neighbours, had been given to her parents. With Gilbert and Betty having no car of their own, the Rector at that time, John Russell, and postmaster, Stan Stamp, set up a transportation service from the village, so that Jane could be visited on a daily basis during her crisis. At **Greatham School**, headmistress Gwen Brooker, ably assisted by teacher Jean Bolam, organised a sponsored walk by the children, in order to raise funds.

Jane has always been grateful for the kindness and generosity of those people in **Greatham** who helped her parents through such a stressful time. She eventually became well enough to get about again, but was unable to return to her studies. A newspaper story, published around that time, reported as follows:

"The village of kindness got its reward yesterday – a young girl's smile. The happiness on the face of 17-year old Jane Coombes told the big-hearted

Pook Cottage, Church Lane, home to Jane's three great aunts

villagers that their efforts had been worthwhile. They had rallied round when student Jane was seriously hurt in a road accident. For five months she lay in hospital, sometimes close to death.

She desperately needed the comfort of her parents at her bedside. But the hospital was thirty miles away from their home and they had no car. That's when the people of **Greatham**, Hampshire, came to the rescue. Every single day, one or another of them called at Jane's home to chauffeur her parents to and from the hospital in Portsmouth.

Now the hospital treatment is over and Jane is back home amongst those same villagers again, saying 'Thank you' by being her old happy self. Postmaster Mr Stanley Stamp, who organised the car rota, said "The day after the accident, people started volunteering to help. Jane's mother, Mrs Betty Coombes, said "I can never forget the kindness. Many of the volunteers hardly knew Jane".

Jane's memories of her young life before the accident remain amazingly vivid, but sadly she now suffers short-term memory loss on an almost daily basis. She is now married to ex-soldier John Rolling and lives at nearby Lindford. When she read about publication of the book, *'A History of Greatham'*, in the local paper, she was delighted to purchase a copy for herself and rekindle memories of her happy childhood days.

Some early memories

Jane seems to remember that it was a Shirley Robinson who was running a playgroup in the village, prior to Sandra Allan. *(This was later confirmed to me by another Shirley (Redpath). Ed.)* After her accident, when Jane found that she was unable to get a job, Sandra was more than happy to let Jane help out at the playgroup for many months. When Jane had previously been at College, she had been a baby-sitter for Sandra, no doubt looking after both young sons, Nigel and Martin, in turn. Another memory that comes back is that Val Russell, the Rector's wife, was instrumental in setting up the original playgroup with Shirley Robinson. Jane recalls that the Russells had two daughters, Lisa and Philippa, along with sons Simon and Mark. Mark proved to have an excellent singing voice, eventually passing exams for a place in one of the country's top choirs.

Betty Trigg had been a **Greatham** Brownie in her younger days but, by the time that Jane was old enough to pursue a similar pastime, the Brownies were defunct. Happily, Mrs Winnie Knott had moved to nearby Liss Forest and opened a Girl Guide pack at **Greatham**, located in the Rectory. Jane remembers that she was appointed patrol leader in charge of Kingfisher Patrol, with Karen Siney one of her patrol; while Rachael Windibank looked after Robin Patrol. Being the senior members, Jane and Rachael would proudly carry the Guides pennant on the monthly church parades. Years later, when Jane had recovered sufficiently from her accident, she returned to the pack as a Guider, then later helped the Brownies alongside Jean

Betty and her mother on a charabanc trip

Turner and Shirley Lilley.

Jane can recall that numbers fell and that the Brownies closed down for a while, until teacher Rita Gerard re-started the pack, assisted by Joyce Gripton and Susan Armitage. In fact, for a little while at least, **Greatham** actually had all four youth organisations, Girl Guides, Brownies, Boy Scouts and Cubs, up and running. At one point, a fund-raising effort between all four organisations raised £250 towards the training of a guide dog for the blind. During Jane's 'Guiding' days, the Baden-Powell movement celebrated sixty years of the founding of the Girl Guides. Gilbert Coombes designed two kneelers for the Church and, between them, the family made the tapestry covers. Jane recalls that John Russell had them put near the altar at the time.

Deal Cottages

Whilst living at Deal Cottages, on Saturday and Sunday afternoons it became traditional for the Coombes family to take a walk through the village. Often, one port of call would be at Swain's Cottage, this when there were still two separate cottages. Here they would stop for a chat 'over the garden fence' with Ernie and Dorothy Collins, who later moved to Tom's Acre Cottage, opposite the Selborne turning. Ernie, more commonly known as Jim, and Dorothy were the parents of Joyce Coffin, who still lives along the Selborne Road. Then they would turn about and make their way down Church Lane to Pook Cottage. That was then the home of Jane's three great aunts, Edie, Emmy and Alice Luff, and Jane says that they always kept the front garden in a very nice condition. Pook Cottage also boasted an arch, over which the summer flowers would grow in profusion. Then their walk would take them further down the lane to Willow Lea, where Jane's grandfather, Fred Trigg, and great-grandfather both lived. She remembers that Mrs Bradley lived in 'the corner house', while Martha and Arthur Randall were also neighbours.

Betty Coombes and Jane at Deal Cottages, 1956

Jane's grandfather had been widowed when his daughter Betty was only a baby, but had then re-married to Kathleen, who had been sent to **Greatham** during the Second World War. Jane recalls that her grandfather used to work at 'a bricklayers in Snailing Lane'. *(Jane also mentions that 'the bricklayers' were not mentioned in 'A History of Greatham' – they certainly would have been if someone had told me about them! Ed.)* Occasionally, the weekend walk would be extended when the family walked across the old 'green lane' that stretches from Church Lane across to the Alton road. There was less traffic to worry about in those days, so they would cross the road and pay a visit to **Greatham Mill Gardens**, in the days when Captain and Mrs Pumphrey still successfully ran the gardens for public display.

Jane also remembers that the 'village bobby' (those were the days!) always lived in the first house in Bakersfield. A PC (Police Constable) Wendon was one such bobby, while his daughter attended the school as an infant alongside Jane. Another incumbent

Peter Gripton

King's Holt Cottage

for a while was a PC Hipkis, who had two daughters. As stated, Jane and her family had lived in one of Deal Cottages (Thele Knapp) when Jane was little, at the opposite end to Amy Pickard, with Mrs Miller in between. As far as Jane can remember, they moved 'up the road' when Jane was around seven years of age, probably during 1963.

King's Holt Cottage

Betty Coombes had gone to work for the Hileys, who lived in the large house, King's Holt, which 'owned' the estate. Prior to that move, Jane remembers going out to pick potatoes, with her mother and 'Vi' Hazel. With the estate cottage becoming vacant, the Coombes' were asked if they would like to move in. Thus, Jane and David were able to use the large estate virtually as their own playground, playing in the fields and woods that surrounded the house. One gate led onto Longmoor Road, just opposite *'Beeleigh'*, a small grocery store run by the Pooleys. *(Mr Pooley later left and returned to what was still then Rhodesia, while Shirley Pooley continued to live in the house for many years, long after it had ceased to be a grocer's. Jim Farrar later ran his photography business from the store – he and Shirley eventually married. Ed)*

The first Rector that Jane can remember was Rex Tyler, who stayed in **Greatham** for eighteen years, from 1948 through until 1966. An old lady by the name of Miss Mills lived in Rectory Close in those days, and Jane's father Gilbert used to do some gardening for her. But she had left by the time that the Russells moved in, on the Rev Tyler's departure. Jane has fond memories of teaching the younger children, including Lisa and Philippa Russell, to draw and make models at Sunday School each week, while Huguette Jenkinson taught the older children.

The annual Church Fete always provided one of the highlights of the year. Jane remembers that her father, along with Jim Collins and Eric Siney and another mate called 'Reggie', would set up the skittles for the bowling competition. The same set of skittles would later be used for the other village fete, the one run by the Cheshire Home at Le Court. **Greatham** had also boasted a Women's Fellowship and Young Wives' group at one time, but by the time that Jane had become old enough to join, the group had closed down! She and her mother, Betty, then joined up with another group, known as *'Dorcas'*, which met regularly for a period, had guest speakers and went on organised outings.

Jane became quite friendly with Albert Baker, the well known 'mouth and foot' artist, from the time that she used to help out in the Le Court workshop. Here she assisted the residents to make wicker trays and baskets, amongst other things. She was always willing to help out in pushing the residents around in their wheelchairs on their outings, or merely for a breath of fresh air on 'play days'. Jane recalls that Mrs Winnie Murphy, who only recently died at the grand old age of ninety-seven, used to be one of the other volunteer helpers at Le Court.

Another pastime recalled by Jane, were

the summer evening fishing trips to 'the bather', located alongside the old pumping station at the back of Wolfmere Lane. *(Although the pumping station has long since disappeared, the 'fishing pond' has been greatly enlarged in recent years and has been officially taken over by a leisure/ angling organisation. Ed.)* Gilbert Coombes was a regular member of what was then Longmoor Fishing Club, while son David became of its junior members. Another member of the club was John Rolling, who was stationed at Longmoor Camp, attached to No.8 Squadron RCT (Royal Corps of Transport). When he returned to the area, on a REME (Royal Electrical and Mechanical Engineers) training course at Bordon, he met up again with Gilbert in the *Silver Birch*. That meeting eventually led to Jane and John getting married, on May 14th 1983. John Russell came back to **Greatham**, especially to take the wedding service.

Despite her short-term memory problems, today Jane can still recall many of the **Greatham** villagers of her early days. One of her earliest school friends was a Jacqueline Patterson, one of a family of four children that lived in Bakersfield and who had lost their mother when they were only young. Also in her year at school was Robert Kemp, one of the large Kemp family that had long been associated with **Greatham**. A girl called Sandra Dow later moved into the village, her father was a fireman at Bordon. Another girl, Melanie Evans, lived with her family in 'The Old Post Office' and she is now a Methodist minister in Petersfield.

Whilst still living in Deal Cottages, Jane recalls that the children of Bakersfield would always build their November 5th bonfire on the green in the centre of the houses. From their garden, Jane's family could watch the fireworks and the glow of the bonfire. Some of the people that Jane later learned had helped her family out, at the time of her dreadful accident, include Ann and Brian Roke, Kathleen, George and Michael Wakeford, Shirley and Pat Redpath, and Pat and Ray Flack, who were then running the village garage.

Jane's father, Gilbert Coombes

A terrible setback

It must have come as a great shock to Jane when her mother Betty died in May 1994. Already suffering as a result of her accident, she now suffered a severe relapse and became very ill again, with epilepsy now being diagnosed. But Jane reckons that she is bound to live to a ripe old age, due to the fact that the hospitals in Portsmouth have already saved her life on three occasions. She still maintains contact with 'Aunty' Amy Pickard, who used to be a neighbour of the Coombes family back in their Deal Cottages days and who grew up with Gilbert Coombes's sisters. In fact Amy had the honour of being bridesmaid to one of them, Lily, who married a soldier and moved away from the village when her husband was 'posted'.

Jane wasn't the first member of the family to suffer in a 'bike accident'. Many years previously, Gilbert's older brother, Albert, had been killed. Despite being an Army dispatch rider, he came off his bike whilst on a trip to Bristol with another **Greatham** resident, Arthur Randall. Gilbert Coombes had been training to become a gardener but, when the Second World War broke out in

Greatham Post Office, *when Stan Stamp was postmaster*

1939, he was recruited as a driver and went on to serve in the Far East. In fact, he was the proud holder of the 'Burma Star'.

Gilbert was one of five children, born to Maurice and Florrie Coombes. Two other children died at a very early age. Apart from the previously mentioned Albert and Lily, Gilbert had two other sisters, Joyce and Phyllis. Gilbert died in January 1999 and the ashes of both Jane's parents now lie together in the churchyard of St John the Baptist, where Jane's own daughter, Joanne Lesley, was christened, following her birth in October 1985.

After the sad departures of her parents, Jane more or less lost touch with the local happenings here in **Greatham**. Most of her 'knowledge' now comes from the pages of the local newspapers, and her thoughts often turn to her happy childhood days whenever passing up 'No Road' (the Woolmer bypass) on the Petersfield bus. However, her interest has recently been revitalised since reading the history book.

*(As the author of that work, I was happy to receive Jane's own story, as seen above, and hope that it may feature in some future update to the history of **Greatham**. Following a plea to her brother David, Jane was also kind enough to provide me with several family photographs, from which I was able to extract some nostalgic pictures of her parents, Betty and Gilbert. Ed.)*

Chapter 10
Keepers Cottage

Back in 1993, a letter was delivered onto the doormat at Keeper's Cottage, just off Church Lane, Greatham. It had been written by Mrs Prue Swatton, now living near Bath in Somerset, members of whose family had lived at the cottage many years previously. The letter read as follows:

"First of all, may I thank you again for allowing my son and I to see Keeper's Cottage and to see how much of the original is still there. Today I have received the photographs that I promised you. They are copies of the originals and show the Corps family and the house as it was. They are for you to keep, should you wish to do so.

*After we left you, we paused at 'Pilgrim's Way', as I felt that this was the cottage 'Robins', to which my grandparents once moved. Again, we were fortunate enough to meet the owner and, when I explained, he said, "This **is** (or was) Robins". So, my son took more photographs, which we can later compare. I have sent them copies of photographs taken in the mid-1930s when, with my parents, we spent holidays there. I presume the reason for the move was that, when the family grew up and left home, they moved to a smaller cottage, to make room for a couple with a family.*

My grandparents left Robins in 1937 or 1938, to live with their daughter in Essex, as they were both then ailing. I can now picture the house, with the copse adjoining, and imagine the cuckoo's call, the pheasants in the lane – and the peace."

It is unfortunate that I only met up with Mrs Chris Beenham, present incumbent of Keeper's Cottage, a short while after my book, *'A History of Greatham'*, had already been published. But Chris kindly furnished me with the above details and also let me copy some photographs that she had collected, showing several previous occupants of Keeper's Cottage.

The Corps family

One photograph, apparently taken in 1901, shows members of the Corps family in all their splendour, arrayed outside the front door of the cottage. Thomas Corps was born on May 4th 1860. He worked as a cowman and agricultural labourer for Sir Heath Harrison of Le Court and the cottage no doubt then belonged to that estate. Thomas snr died on December 12th 1945 at the grand old age of eighty-five. His wife Caroline (nee Chitty) was born on September 12th 1856 and died on February 8th 1940. The couple was married at nearby Empshott parish church in 1882. Also shown on the photograph are their three sons, Walter,

Keeper's Cottage, Church Lane, c.1920

William and Thomas jnr – the latter then aged fourteen and shown with his hand on his hip. This young lad became father to Prue (Prudence), who wrote the letter above. Last on the photograph is daughter Martha Elizabeth, known to all as Pat! A second photograph, taken from an original postcard (very popular in those days!), shows Caroline Corps feeding some chickens outside the cottage, alongside another lady, sometime between 1918 and 1923.

*(Another group of photographs bears witness to Keeper's Cottage having been home to the Fry family in later years – the same Frys who figure in the chapters about the Hayward and Marie families, mentioned elsewhere in the **Greatham** history. Having seen the pictures, which are all relatively small, Jackie and Bill Marie discussed them with Bill's sister Pearl and, between them, they were able to identify most of their earlier family members. Prominent amongst them are Grandfather and Granny Fry, many of their children, and Florence Hayward, who later married into the Fry family. Ed.)*

Keeper's Cottage sits down towards the bottom of Church Lane, but is just about invisible from the lane, unless one ventures along the separate track that leads off at a footpath sign. Martin and Chris Beenham have lived there for around thirty years now, having purchased the house from a Mrs Galbraith, a widow who lived there with her son, who is believed to have run a taxi service at the time.

It is believed that the house – or cottage – was built sometime between 1840 and 1860. Looking at the photograph of Keeper's when the Corps family lived there, one can see that there had been an added extension at one end of the house. In front of that extension are a coal store and boiler room, while a long porch runs along the front of the house, but all these have long since disappeared. Chris relates that the porch shut out a lot of light, making the house very dark inside. The boiler room had also been converted into a kitchen, but one could actually see through the walls and into the garden.

Some original interior doors had been covered, first with plywood and then that sticky-backed vinyl, believed to be called 'Fablon'. Access to 'upstairs', was by a staircase that more closely resembled a ladder! At one place upstairs are the remains of the original 'wattle and daub' construction, while one outside wall remains uncovered by any modern material, showing a fine ironstone pattern. Two downstairs windows provide the evidence that the house once belonged to a gamekeeper, as the windows still retain the original iron bars that were obviously designed to keep out anyone inclined to steal one of the gamekeeper's guns. They also show up well on the 1901 photograph, so have well stood the test of time.

Footnote 1

I was delighted to make contact with Prue Swatton at a later date and she asked me to send her a copy of the **Greatham** history. Her father, Thomas Corps (jnr) was born in 1887 and lived a long life of some ninety years. Prior to the First World War he was an Evangelist in the Church Army, conducting a mission at Bursledon, just outside Southampton. It was here that he met and married Florence Humby. Florence was five years older than her husband, but lived almost as long a life, which ended in 1974. Prue, herself born in 1923, has two sons, Andrew and John, both of whom are keen railway enthusiasts.

Another pleasant surprise came a few days after I had dispatched the book to Prue. I had a phone call from her cousin, Caroline Blackwell, now living in the pretty Suffolk countryside in a small place called Clare. Caroline recalls her grandmother, after whom she was named, walking all the way down to Liss for her shopping, whilst pushing a pram. Caroline, who was born in 1929, also requested a copy of the **Greatham** history and it is wonderful to know that people still retain such happy memories of our village that they want to read all about it!

The Corps family at Keeper's Cottage c.1901

Footnote 2

At the beginning of June 2004, I was delighted to hear again from Prue. She had been taking her time to read carefully through **'A History of Greatham'**, which brought so many fond memories of her own happy childhood days, visiting her grandparents in Church Lane. She had also been able to find a copy of a photograph that she herself had taken *"with (her) Brownie box-camera, when (she) was about twelve years old"*. The picture certainly proves the story she told in her 1993 letter, because it shows both of her paternal grandparents, Thomas and Caroline Corps, as well as her own parents, Thomas and Florence Corps. Prue estimates that it was taken around 1935, when her grandparents were living at Robins, but the photograph gives little indication of an exact location.

Describing her memories of that photograph, Prue wrote as follows:

"Grandfather's hands are those of a man who milked cows, laid hedges, hoed fields of root crops and all that was necessary on the estate of Sir Heath Harrison. By this time, my father (Thomas jnr.) had served with the Royal Engineers (RE), in the Persian Gulf, during the First World War".

Prue later enlarged upon this by writing again, with the information that her father's World War I service was with the Inland Water Transport section of the RE. The section conveyed supplies by riverboat to those troops fighting in Mesopotamia, now more infamously known as Iraq. Thomas Corps sailed up the River Tigris and was well acquainted with the cities of Basra and Baghdad, still trouble spots on the world stage to this very day. He also went on to serve in India.

After that war of 1914-18, Prue's parents, on behalf of the Church Army, ran a hostel for limbless ex-servicemen in London. Eventually they moved down to the fine and famous old city of Bath, where they ran a men's hostel. They gave this up shortly before Prue was born, her father then obtaining a secretarial post. In their declining years, her parents went to live with Prue and she nursed them both until their final days.

Chapter 11
A Simple Life by Phyllis Workman

Early childhood memories

The first house I remember living in was a converted railway carriage, with a veranda fitted along its length, situated at the top of a field. My father had left the Army soon after I was born and moved back to King's Heath, Birmingham, and this was the best accommodation he could find for us. We had the whole field to play in, except for the corner where the chickens were. In wet weather we played on the veranda. My father was a blacksmith and worked in one of the factories (*Cadbury's* I think, but I am not sure). I know my uncle worked there and we did occasionally go to see the horses being shod.

One day when I was about five years old, my brother Frank persuaded me to go out of the field to go and meet John, son of a neighbour, who had just bought a motor bike and had promised Frank a ride in the sidecar. We walked to the top of the road, but no sign of John anywhere, so we walked on and on. By this time I was crying, because I was tired and knew we were lost. A lady asked why I was crying and took us to a police station; by this time we were three miles away from home. We were taken into a large room, where a policeman was asking where we had come from, when a voice boomed out, *"Get those so-and-so children out from here, there is a flogging going on"*. I think I had a nightmare that night! Another time, I was walking to school with Frank and said I didn't want to go to school, as I didn't like the teacher. So Frank said, *"Do what I do - go and play in the fields until it's time to go home"*. I did just that, but the only trouble was that I got bored and went home. When I told my mother I had been to school, she knew I hadn't, but she did let me stay at home for the rest of the day. But I had to promise never to do that again.

By this time, my mother was diagnosed with breast cancer, so was often not well, although we children were not aware of it at the time. But we did move house, to about a mile away; this was a red brick cottage with upstairs rooms, a novelty to us. We still went to the same school and Sunday school. My sister Gertrude, though called Trudy by us all, and I joined the Brownies and were also allowed to go to Saturday morning cinema, which showed special children's films. Occasionally my mother would take me into Birmingham to the *John Lewis* store, where I would happily spend time going up and down on the escalators. These were quite a new addition. Surprisingly, I was never told off, I think perhaps it persuaded people it was quite safe to go on!

In the summer, we were taken to Sutton Park and Cannon Hill Park, it was always fun playing in the water there. Also, one of my father's cousins owned a pony and trap milk float and sometimes, in the holidays, he would take us out on his round. He had found an ideal place to leave us to play in a shallow stream, where we could catch 'tiddlers' while he carried on with his round. My brother Frank would often go across the road to help (?) Mr Bird, who owned the boathouse; he usually came home wet through, after falling in the canal. My Mother used to make ice cream at the weekends, to sell to the people going past on the barges. My uncle would collect large lumps of ice, used for keeping the ice cream cold, as nobody owned freezers in those days.

Life changed dramatically when I was seven years old; my father fell through a roof at work, breaking both arms and a leg, and was in hospital for some time. Also, my sister developed double pneumonia, while my mother was in and out of hospital with her cancer. My aunt came up from Sussex to look after us. One nice day in October, we children were allowed to go to see my mother, who had been wheeled outside into the sunshine. Sadly, she died a few days later, aged only thirty-three.

The following spring, my father, who was not fit enough to go back to work, decided to buy a chicken farm in Hampshire. This was a big upheaval, as life there was entirely different for all of us - my aunt came too. The school was three miles away, in Ropley, and we had to walk there and back. We used to play about on the way and often met the school inspector, who was on his way to see why we were not at school! We were often so late that we were marked absent.

Dad had bought an old car, a *'Singer'* with an open top, but that was only used to take eggs down to Lee-on-the-Solent, where he had customers, so he couldn't spare the time to take us to school. I disliked that school, as the other children poked fun at me for having a Birmingham (Brummie) accent. Once, we were taking my Gran, who was visiting us, out in the car for a picnic, with all of us piled in the car. There was food and drink in the boot, and a bottle of homemade apple juice suddenly made a terrific bang as the cork flew out, frightening us all. Of course, Dad braked quickly, thinking it was the engine, but luckily no damage was done.

On fine Sunday evenings in summer, the congregation of the nearby chapel used to gather on our front lawn for their evening service, a tradition started by the previous owner. We children were told to stay clean and tidy and make sure we behaved ourselves. On our way to the Sunday School, at the chapel in Monkwood, among the trees was an oak tree which were told it took ten men with their arms outstretched to go round. I never found out if that was true - but it was certainly a very big tree! I also remember Frank getting into trouble again, swinging on the back of a hay-cart and getting his foot caught in the wheel, ending up in hospital with a broken ankle.

After a few months, my aunt decided she needed to go back to work. I don't think the chicken farm was very successful, as my father was left to look after three children as well as the chickens, which he found impossible to do. Trudy and I ended up in a small children's home in Alton, while Frank went to one in Basingstoke. It meant that Trudy and I only saw him once a month, when he came on the train to visit us, on the day that we were allowed visitors. Usually Dad and Auntie Maud came too. The home we were in was a large house, divided into two separate units, with twelve children in each and a 'mother figure' in charge. The strict routine was rather difficult after the life of freedom that we had before. We went to the local school, which I liked better than the Ropley one.

On Saturday mornings we all had jobs to do around the house. Mine was cleaning silver - all the knives, forks and spoons etc, which seemed a never-ending task. But in the afternoon, the older girls were allowed to take girls over eight years old to the cinema, if there was a children's film on. Shirley Temple was a favourite and, if there was a queue, one of the older girls would go up to the box office and tell them we were from the home and had to get back by a certain time. Then we would be taken up to a seat in 'the circle', a great treat, and also be given ice cream during the interval. Usually it was bread and jam for tea, unless it was someone's birthday - then we would have trifle and cake. In the summer we sometimes had salad, which had to be carefully washed to make sure there were no 'creepy crawlies' or slugs in the lettuce.

A move to Greatham

In August 1936, my father married my Aunt Maud and they rented a house in Pine Villas, Liphook Road, in ***Greatham***. Frank, Trudy and I joined them just before Christmas. I was then ten years of age,

Peter Gripton

Mr Kirby's shop, Longmoor Road

while Frank was eleven and Trudy was just eight. I remember that my first days at **Greatham School** were a little daunting, as all my teachers had, up until then, been of the female variety and I was now put into Mr Wain's class. He was also the headmaster and had no hesitation in wielding the cane on the hands of those children he caught misbehaving. Nowadays he'd probably be locked up for mistreating them! My brother Frank was often in trouble, being something of a tearaway in those days. I managed to get caught once, along with two other girls, flicking paper pellets across the room with a ruler. Our punishment was that we had to stand under the clock, which was in the hall behind the folding screen that separated Mr Wain's classroom from the hall. I think our pride was hurt more than our hands though.

Another teacher, Miss Perry, would occasionally take the class out across the nearby fields for nature walks, so we actually did learn the names of a lot of the wild flowers that grew locally. We also had to write a sentence about 'something to do with nature' that we had seen on our way to school every morning. Miss Perry also taught needlework to the girls in our class, while Mr Wain had the boys outside, 'gardening' in a patch of ground by the side of the playground. Every so often, an inspector used to call at the school to examine our knowledge of Religion and, if we had answered the questions to his satisfaction, we would be given the rest of the day off. I also have a vague recollection of being let out from school to follow the beagles, when they met for 'the Hunt' at Captain Coryton's manor house, but we later had to report back to school in case anyone got lost. When we were either twelve or thirteen, once a fortnight we girls went off to Petersfield School to learn cookery and domestic science, while the boys, I believe, had carpentry lessons at Liss School.

Eileen Shepherd, the village blacksmith's eldest daughter, used to come into the school to play the piano for our singing lessons. Mr Wain's favourite songs seemed to be *"Glorious Devon"*, *"Who is Sylvia? What is she?"* and *"Who'll buy my lavender, fresh gathered lavender?"* to which the boys used to sing *"Who'll buy my cabbage stumps, fresh gathered cabbage stumps?"* - much to the amusement of the girls of course, until it was stopped with the promise of the cane. Despite his disciplinary threats, Mr Wain was a very good teacher and well respected. I for one have always been very grateful for the excellent grounding we had in the 'Three R's' and also a good basic knowledge of history, geography and general knowledge.

On Sundays, Trudy and I attended 'Sunday school' in the Methodist Chapel in Liphook Road, which I think has since been re-named Longmoor Road. The chapel, built of corrugated metal and irreverently called by some the 'Tin Tabernacle', itself has long disappeared to make way for housing. Mr Ansell, who lived in the next house down the road, and Mr Kirkby from the bicycle shop, took it in turns to run this, while Gladys Shepherd, the blacksmith's younger daughter, played the piano for us. *(In my book, 'A History of Greatham', a photograph shows 'Busty' Ansell standing outside the old chapel – my home, Chapel House, now stands on the same site. Ed.)*

In the summer, after Sunday school had ended, we would dash up to the sports field, to the left of Applepie Hill on the moor, where the Army reserves, who came to Longmoor for their fortnight's training, usually held a sports afternoon. If we were lucky enough, we would arrive in time to enter the children's races, where all those who entered would be given either sweets or ice cream. As we did not get many sweets at home in those days, this was a real treat.

Saturday mornings would be spent collecting fir cones and pieces of wood, which would be used to light the fire under 'the copper' (boiler). This would heat the water for our baths, taken in a tin bath in front of the kitchen range, whilst also providing the water ready for the traditional Monday's washing-day. There were no such luxuries as washing machines or bathrooms in those days! Even the toilet was just a partitioned off corner of the outdoors shed, with a wooden seat and a bucket underneath; a trapdoor at the back meant that the bucket could be taken out and emptied in the garden. I recall that it was very cold and draughty, using the toilet in the winter!

My father had an allotment at Blackmoor and sometimes we would walk over the moor to help him. We would also go to Mr Kirby's shop to pay the paper money and hopefully buy a pennyworth of sweets. *(This shop ended its days as a photographer's studio, run by Jim Farrar. Ed.)* Children's shoes always seemed to be in need of repair and these would be taken up to Mr Cumber's house. He lived a little way up Benham's Lane, at the top end of the village, and would mend shoes for a reasonable price.

When I was eleven years old I joined the Girl Guides, which was then run by Miss Ingles, an elderly lady who lived in the house by the side of the Woolmer Hotel. Her helper with the Guides was a younger lady but I cannot remember her name. We used to meet in the old school on a Saturday and I thought I looked 'the cat's whiskers' in my uniform. Unfortunately, Miss Ingles decided to finish the Guides after the bombs fell on Longmoor and Mr Gilburd's farm, as she didn't feel she could take the responsibility for our safety. We had been due to give a concert in Mr Hope's garden on the evening of the day that the bombs fell. This was cancelled when we were told not to gather in groups, in case the German bombers came back.

I remember Trudy and I, along with one or two friends, once walking to the 'Zigzag' path at Selborne to gather primroses. We took a picnic with us and later, walking back through the lanes to Blackmoor, we arrived home very weary with the primroses somewhat wilted. We never tried walking it again and did not go there again until a year or two later, by which time we had obtained bicycles, second-hand ones, from some Army families being posted abroad from Longmoor.

During the summer holidays of 1938, Trudy and I decided to go fruit picking at *Whangerei Fruit Farm* at Liss Forest, in order to earn some pocket money. We were given the job of picking red currants first of all, then went on to strawberries and black currants. We were very tired by the time we walked home again in the evening but it was worth it. We were absolutely thrilled when we received our pay packet at the end of the week; it was over £2, which was a lot of money in those days. Quite a lot of the fruit pickers were from the East End of London; they were always very kind to us and we enjoyed the experience. They were going off to the hop fields in Kent after the fruit picking finished, while we were heading back to school.

'The Bather' was cleaned out, along with the small pool at the side of the main pool, by the Army, sometime during 1938 or 1939. Children were allowed to use it on Saturday mornings and we learned to swim there. Usually there was a soldier present on duty, in case we got into difficulties. On the way home we would collect bilberries, which grew in profusion along the side of the lane, at the top of Applepie Hill. These would then be made into a tart for Sunday lunch.

Just behind 'the Bather', somewhere near where the new bypass is now providing its incessant noise, that fascinating plant

Frank Smith Apprentice soldier at Arborfield, 1942

'Sundew' used to grow - I have never seen it growing wild anywhere else. Also, cotton plants grew in the marshy area to the right of Smith's Lane. Towards the end of the year, as Christmas approached, Frank and I would go down to the woods to get a Christmas tree, taking care to avoid being spotted by Mr Keen, the Range Warden. We were told that he had eleven sons and one daughter - I think her name was Florence, but I am not really sure of that. She was still a pupil at **Greatham School** when I first went there, but the boys had all left school by that time.

On Sunday evenings in the summer, when the weather was nice, we would all go for a walk, with a stop at *'The Deer's Hut'* at Grigg's Green or *'The Temple'* at Liss Forest, so that we could all have a drink.

As my father worked for the Army at Longmoor Camp, we children were allowed free rides on the military trains; so we often went up to Bordon, sometimes to the cinema there, or just for the ride. We also went to Liss to collect meat from the butcher's shop, even though meat was delivered twice a week. We were also allowed to go to the cinema at Longmoor, I believe a film called *'The Lady Vanishes'* was made there in 1937, while another film of a train crash was later made on the Longmoor Military Railway line about 1955. *(That would have been 'Bhowani Junction', starring Ava Gardner and Stewart Granger. Ed.)*

1937 was 'Coronation Year' for King George VI and his Queen, Elizabeth, who went on to live until her hundredth year as our beloved 'Queen Mum'. I recall that all of the village children were presented with a 'Coronation mug', and it was also memorable for me as the year that my half-brother Ronald was born.

The outbreak of war

Life changed a great deal for everyone after the war broke out in 1939. My father re-enlisted in the Army and only came home when on leave, although he did eventually get posted to the Farnham area, so that we then saw him more often. Then my brother Frank went off to the Army Apprentices' School at Arborfield, up near Reading in Berkshire. *(A photograph of Frank, dated December 1941, shows him in the Service Dress (SD) of the time and wearing the cap-badge of the Royal Army Ordnance Corps (RAOC). The following year, the Royal Electrical and Mechanical Engineers (REME) was formed, and those boys still at Arborfield would have been automatically transferred into this new technical Corps. I myself joined the same Army school at Arborfield, in 1956. Ed.)* It was very quiet at home without the pair of them. We were all issued with gas masks, which we had to carry around with us whenever we went out. My young brother Ron was issued with a *'Mickey Mouse'* mask, which he hated! We also had to keep identity cards with us wherever we went and I can still remember my number 'EEQC44/4'.

On the morning that the bombs fell on **Greatham**, we were still in bed. Trudy and I dashed across to the window to see what all the noise was about, just in time to see clouds of earth fly up in the air from the bomb that fell in Mr Gilburd's orchard. When we realised what was happening, we beat a hasty retreat to the cellar, which had been reinforced with large wooden planks. We also slept down there when the air raids started at night.

Mr Walters, the baker, had a large hut in the grounds of his shop. This was opened for Sunday evening services, to which all denominations were welcomed. Mr and Mrs Tarr and their daughter Ruth, who was a friend of mine, used to go there, so Trudy and I were invited along to join them. Although it was run mainly for the benefit of the soldiers, we helped with the teas, which I think were free in those days. Inside, the hut was divided in two; one half was used for the services and the other was a recreation room with a snooker table, table tennis and darts and so on. This was open every evening from 6.30 until 8.30 p.m. Then there would be a short service until 9 p.m. Mr Willday from Liphook was in charge and a Miss Moss played the organ.

With the looming threat of a German invasion of the south coast, large concrete pillars were put halfway across the Liphook road, near the old chapel. There was also a pillbox built for either soldiers or the Home Guard to help defend Longmoor from any invading troops. I can remember that soldiers were often spotted in the ditches by the side of the road at night, but I'm not sure whether they were on duty or just sleeping out from the Camp!

Going to work

I left school at the age of fourteen in 1940 and, for a few short weeks worked for Mrs Moseley (Bill Moseley's mother) at their shop at Longmoor Camp. This was just a wooden hut by the side of the square, which sold a lot of odds-and-ends including needles, cottons, buttons, cleaning materials, socks etc but mainly cigarettes and sweets, to the soldiers who were stationed there. I think that was before the days of rationing, as I remember that Mrs Moseley often gave me a bar of chocolate. Unfortunately, the shop closed shortly after I had started working there.

After that, I went to work for the Postmaster, mainly delivering telegrams around the camp, but I was not very keen on that. My stepmother thought that 'being in service' was a good career for girls, so she found me a job as a housemaid at *'Leydene'*, which was Lady Peel's house at East Meon. My work there was mainly making sure that the many guestrooms were kept clean and tidy. I also remember waiting in the broom cupboard, on the landing near Lady's Peel's room, for the lady herself to go down to dinner, often sitting at the long table in the dining room all on her own. Then I could make sure her room was tidy and turn the bed down. Lady Peel must have been rather a lonely lady, as the only other people in the house were the servants, these being a butler, a footman/chauffeur, a cook, kitchen maid and scullery maid, a housekeeper and two housemaids. We were all very much 'below stairs' staff, apart from the butler, who we only saw when something was not quite to his liking.

When the dreadful bombing of Portsmouth started, a dormitory was set up in the cellar for the female staff. It was unfortunate if anyone needed the toilet in the night! It meant a journey up two flights of stairs and along a long corridor in the dark. Because of the blackout, with just a torch for illumination, it was all very creepy. Eventually, the Royal Navy requisitioned the house in 1941, so I was out of a job once more and I went back home to **Greatham**.

After trying one or two other domestic jobs, and deciding that I didn't enjoy it very much, I went to work at Petersfield, for *A.G. Suthers*. He was an electrical contractor who, besides running his own electrical business, had a small factory where he employed about twelve girls working on Radar equipment for the Admiralty. In my section, each girl was given a plan and asked to assemble and wire up racks six feet tall and eighteen inches wide, each one taking about a month to complete. An Admiralty inspector would arrive once a month to check the assembled racks. That work was quite varied and interesting, although we never did see any Radar actually working. That Admiralty contract came to an end sometime in 1947.

*Phyllis and Malcolm married at **Greatham** in 1956*

I used to cycle the six or so miles from **Greatham** to Petersfield and back every day, until the traffic became too heavy with the build up of troops and equipment going to Rowlands Castle, in preparation for 'D-Day' in June 1944. It was no longer very safe to be on a bike, so I would cycle only as far as Liss Forest and catch a *Cartwright's* bus from there, as there was no early morning bus from **Greatham**. The first Aldershot bus didn't arrive in Petersfield until 8.15 and we had to start work at 8 a.m. and then work right through until finishing at 5.30 p.m. It was a lovely ride home on an evening when the sun was shining.

During the war, we very rarely went to the main part of the village, as I was then working and Trudy was at Petersfield High School. Our entertainment was mostly confined to the Camp cinema at first but, in 1941, my stepmother decided to let out the two front rooms to a soldier and his wife. She had made friends with them and they were trying to find accommodation near to the camp. This proved lucky for me, as the soldier played in the Longmoor Military Band and also the Dance Band, so I was allowed to accompany his wife to a lot of the functions where the band played. These included dances and band concerts at Longmoor and other military establishments around the district, as well as fetes in nearby villages. I was always sure of a lift home but, looking back now, I am surprised that no one ever queried why we were travelling in military transport! That was an extra bonus in those days, as most youngsters had to walk home if they went out at night.

Returning to a normal life

After the war ended in 1945, life was suddenly very quiet again, so I went to stay with a friend. She and her mother had left their house in Portsmouth, to live in the relative safety of **Greatham** when the bombing of the dockyards started. They were now going back to the city of Portsmouth to live and I was invited to join them. I travelled back to Petersfield by train every day to work. I stayed with them for two years before moving back to **Greatham**, when Mr Suthers' contract with the Admiralty finished. I then started working in Blackmoor Post Office for Mr & Mrs Burridge. I helped with the Post Office work, as well as in the shop. Rationing was well in force then, so butter, cheese etc had to be weighed out carefully.

I was happy to be back among the village people again. While there, I made friends with Pat Bandford, whose parents ran the *Woolmer Hotel* at that time. Pat's half-brother, Don Dunning, kept pigs at the back of the hotel. Pat and I joined the darts club in the public bar, something that would have been unheard of before the war. But women had proved how invaluable they could be in all walks of life during the war, and the old days of 'women in their place' had gone forever.

I also joined the Church choir and began to have many interesting discussions on subjects ranging from music to cures for colds and even science, which I knew very little about! These subjects I discussed with Willy and Edgar Redman, while walking down the road after Church. My brother Frank married Hazel Lacey (sister of Elsie Collins) in 1948.

They lived at Sandpit Cottages, next door to Mr and Mrs Tarr, until they went abroad with the Army. Later on, I joined the WRAF, and during my service with them, I met Malcolm Workman, my future husband. We were married in **Greatham Church** in 1956 and went to live in a small village in the lovely Cotswolds area of Gloucestershire.

That lasted until 1999, when we moved south to Dorchester, Dorset, to be nearer to my younger son, his wife and now his two small sons aged two and four. My greatest pleasure is to see them all at weekends. My elder son is now living in Washington DC, in the United States, with his family. Sadly, Gerald died only a few months after we had moved to Dorset.

I still have many happy memories of growing up in **Greatham**, with the freedom to walk in the woods and roam across the moors, picking the kingcups that grew by the river, and generally enjoying the once peaceful countryside. It makes me realise how lucky we were to live in such a lovely area of Hampshire.

Footnote

My sister Trudy married an Australian and has been living in Brisbane for the last forty-five years. Three of her children have visited me over the past few years. Ron is also in Australia but in Perth, on the opposite side of that vast continent, where he has been for thirty-six years and he has now retired.

Dorchester is a very nice town to live in; there are several ways I can walk into town from my house, most of them through avenues of trees. The Bowling Club is only a few minutes walk away and I manage to play about three times a week and also belong to the WI. I have often been back to **Greatham** over the last fifty years and still hear news of people I knew, from either Elsie or Hazel. I did come to the school reunion a few years ago and enjoyed meeting a few people I knew. My very best wishes to any one who remembers me or any member of my family. I have really enjoyed writing down these memories of my happy days in dear old **Greatham**.

(The above memoirs by Phyllis Workman came about as a result of her being sent a copy of 'A History of Greatham'. She was so delighted to rekindle her own cherished memories of earlier days in the village that she contacted me to say 'thank you'. There then came a mutual agreement that she would write down some of her own thoughts and that I would ultimately edit them into what you find above. Ed.)

Frank Smith (3rd from left) married Hazel Lacey in 1948, at a double wedding. Hazel's sister, Joan married Stanley Jones

Peter Gripton

Chapter 12
Greatham Mill Gardens

In October 2004, the EHDC (East Hants District Council) awards for Conservation and Design were made. Highly commended, under the 'Natural Environment' classification were the gardens at Greatham Mill, for "restoration of gardens, which had been originally created by Mrs Frances Pumphrey between the 1950s and 1980s".

I contacted Elaine and John Graves at **Greatham Mill** and John kindly undertook to put together the following update on progress since taking over the ownership:

*"The gardens at **Greatham Mill** were originally created by Mrs Frances Pumphrey. Although she had no formal training, she began gardening here in the 1950s and became well known as a plants-woman. The garden was built up, over the next thirty years, into a cottage garden on the grand scale and, in its heyday, was featured on various radio and television programmes, including 'Gardener's World'.*

*In 1987, it was included in Alvide Lees-Milne and Rosemary Very's book 'The new Englishwoman's garden' and, more recently in 'Gardens of inspiration', in which Dan Pearson describes how he became inspired by this 'larger than life cottage garden', while working there on his Saturday job. Sadly, in the late 1980s, in the period leading up to and following Frances Pumphrey's death, the garden was neglected and became very overgrown. Having bought **Greatham***

Greatham Mill today

Mill in December 1998, Elaine and John Graves spent their first year renovating the house – then began work on the garden in 2000, when they moved in.

The aim in this has been both to restore the best of Mrs Pumphrey's design and planting schemes, as well as adding some of our own. In general, this has been a three-stage process; firstly clearing away weeds and overgrowth; secondly discovering what is there or should be there; then, finally, either pruning or replacing as necessary. As Mrs Pumphrey always declared that she 'kept it all up there, in her head', and never wrote anything down, there were no records of any planting schemes. We were helped in working out what could have been the 'original design' by Brian Davis. As a nurseryman, he had supplied Mrs Pumphrey with many of her shrubs and therefore knows the garden very well.

The biggest single change has been the coppicing of the alders running up the riverbank, which has opened up the views to 'The Hangers' behind. Having been advised that the old rockery and alpine bed would be impossible to restore, it has been replaced with a swimming pool. A flat paved area, immediately to the rear of the house, and the overhead electricity cable that used to be here, has been removed. Other ground-works have included uncovering and rebuilding the millstream sluice, rebuilding the Mill tailrace wall and water beds, dredging out the old sluice pond and rough-landscaping the remains of the millpond. We have also built the herb garden that Frances Pumphrey always planned to make.

A large amount of replanting has also been accomplished, either as replacements or additions. This ranges from tulip bulbs to cherry trees and, as the garden was always described as 'a spring garden', to extend its range, this has included a large number of clematis and over one hundred replacement roses. Having now opened the garden to the public again, under the 'National Gardens' scheme, the most rewarding thing is to have heard the comments of visitors who knew Mrs Pumphrey about 'how pleased she would be with how it is all now looking'."

Chapter 13
John Cooke

In the first half of March 2005, having just returned from attending my daughter's wedding on the Caribbean island of St Lucia, I was pleasantly surprised – and delighted – to receive the following letter from a John Cooke of Northamptonshire, which read as follows:

"My sister, Mrs Jill Scott, of Heather Drive, Lindford, sent to me for Christmas a copy of your most interesting book, 'A History of Greatham'. I am writing to thank you for the pleasure it has given me, both in looking back at the pictures and reading the text. It has brought back memories of my childhood in Wrecclesham and my very frequent visits to my grandparents, Mr and Mrs Cooke, who lived at what was then called 'Sunnyside'. Their house appears several times in your book, most prominently on page 132, where it is the first house on the left. I well remember that gate, which had dropped on its hinges and needed lifting up to make with the gatepost (a challenge for me as a small child) and, if not lifted, left a deep gouge in the soft sandy soil!

*The book makes several references to my great-grandfather Henry Trigg, whose daughter Mary Elizabeth (known as Polly) married Archibald Henry Gilbert of Stedham, near Midhurst, in about 1907. I am enclosing a copy of the sepia-tone picture of the wedding party. This shows Deal Farmhouse as it was then, which may be of interest to the present occupants. (Sue and Alan Booton. Ed.) The Vicar of **Greatham** is in the picture, on the right in the back row, but I do not know his name. (Records would indicate that this was Cecil Francis Luttrell-West. Ed.)*

They (the Gilberts) made their home in Stedham and their eldest daughter, my mother Kathleen, married John (known as Jack) Cooke in 1932 or 1933. I was born at Whitehill in 1937 – they moved, with Jill and infant me, to Wrecclesham shortly after my birth. I was baptised at Blackmoor Church, in that lovely old Alfred Waterhouse building, funded along with the school etc by Roundell Palmer, Lord Selborne.

I well remember visits to Sunnyside during the latter years of World War Two and the late Forties, bringing home on the single-decker (Dennis) Aldershot & District Number 6 buses, bags full of garden produce grown in Sunnyside's fertile, grey sandy soil. Walks across Longmoor Common with my grandfather were a further feature of the visits and I well recall him making a catapult for me when I was about twelve years old – and then a pupil of Farnham Grammar School.

*The pictures of **Greatham Church** similarly brought back later memories, as I played the organ there at my grandmother's funeral service. A friend of my parents, a Mrs Flander, lived in one of the cottages on the other side of the A325 (whence we went for tea and a sixpence!). Her daughter Lily later married a Brian Matthews and they moved to Hawkley. She had been my mother's bridesmaid at the Stedham wedding. Should I be back that way, which is less likely now that my sister Jill is moving to Fareham soon, I must look at what remains of the first **Greatham Church**.*

Thank you again for the enjoyment your book has brought me - I shall read it on and off for many months to come, of that I'm sure!"

Talk of coincidences! Very shortly after receiving the above letter, I was visiting old friend Tim Gould in Snailing Lane, and we got to chatting about a road route up to Lincolnshire, if I remember correctly. I think Tim was going up that way to look at a tractor at the time. The route Tim had picked up via one of those computer guides mentioned Wellingborough (Northants) – which is where John Cooke now lives. I told Tim about this minor coincidence and he told me a little tale of his own. A few years previously, he and his wife Helen had been away on holiday in Sorrento, Italy. One evening they were standing on the veranda of *'The Royale'* hotel, looking out across the sea, and got chatting with another English chap – none other than the above John Cooke!

During the conversation, in typically English fashion, the chat got around to *'Where do you live?'* and of course Tim mentioned **Greatham** as his adopted home village (Tim's an Essex lad by birth). He was quite surprised when John then told him that he used to visit the village here to visit his grandparents, some fifty-odd years ago. But an even bigger shock awaited - the cottage known to John as *'Sunnyside'* was no less than the same *'Bracken Cottage'*, obviously renamed over the intervening years, that Helen and Tim had moved into when they first arrived in **Greatham** in 1974! The old saying that *'It's a small world'* has never been so true

Chapter 14
Jack Dunn

I'd just returned from a summer holiday in Cornwall on the last day of July (2004) and been sent to replenish stocks at the local supermarket, when I happened to spot Brenda Dunn, along with her daughter Jennifer. I must confess that I hadn't seen Jennifer for a number of years, probably not since I worked in *'The Silver Birch'* during the early Seventies. I started to make some joking comment about something or other, but the look on Brenda's face stopped me in my tracks. *"I'm afraid I've got some bad news, Pete"*, she said, then told me that her husband Jack had died just a few days previously. Jack hadn't been very well for quite some time but, whenever I had dropped in to see him, there had always been a warm welcome, usually accompanied by many a quip or joke. Thus it was that on Friday 6th August, along with a **Greatham Church** full of mourners, I sat and listened to some of the many tributes paid to Jack, during his funeral service.

Huguette Jenkinson, a lay-reader in her own right, officiated at the service and gave some flavour of the man; this was later added to, firstly by Simon Sillence, an old friend of Jack's from the local Royal Naval Association (RNA), and then, movingly, by his grandson David. Simon's eulogy was later reproduced on the front page of an issue of the local RNA newsletter, 'Up Spirits', and is given in full below:

"We are here to celebrate the life of Jack Dunn, the Jolly Sailor. I first saw Jack one evening at the 'Jolly Sailor' pub in Petersfield, sometime in the 1970s – not in person, but his image was painted on the pub's signboard. Unbeknown to me, I would later see the man in person, as he served at the meat counter in the Gateway supermarket. His ready smile, wit and charm won over many a young mother and her toddlers, as he became known as the 'Jolly Butcher'.

Jack had joined the Navy at the age of seventeen years, not long after the outbreak of World War II. He trained at Whale Island in Pompey, first as a gunnery rating, then later as a 'hard hat' diver. This was a job that involved a great deal of danger, a physically and mentally demanding job, one that took courage and tenacity to do, often in total darkness, in cold and inhospitable waters.

He touched the lives of many of us, as those gathered here today can testify. One such event was Jack's diving, in great secrecy, on the wreck of the battleship 'Royal Oak', sunk by Kapitan Prien of U-boat U47 at Scapa Flow, with the loss of many lives. Among them was the brother of Ivy Howard, one of the congregation here today.

In the Pacific, on board the aircraft carrier 'Formidable', Jack survived kamikaze attacks by Japanese aircraft, intent on sinking his ship. In the same theatre of war, in a sister carrier 'Indomitable', he served alongside shipmate Malcolm Meech, another here today.

At the formation of the Liss and District Branch of the RNA, Jack and Brenda were among the founder members, along with Tommy and Ivy Howard, Malcolm and Jean Meech – their lives intertwined by their service to the Crown and the Royal Navy.

Jack always referred to me as 'Deeps', an affectionate nickname between fellow divers. We at Liss are proud and humbled to have known our shipmate

Jack. The world is a little sadder for the 'crossing of the bar' of a sailor's sailor but, above all, we will remember Jack Dunn as the 'Jolly Sailor'".

Simon later kindly gave me permission to use the eulogy above, for which I am most grateful. I also reproduce grandson David's words below:

"My grandfather, Jack Dunn, was born in 1923 in the North East but, in 1925, Jack's father, a Royal Engineer, was posted to Bordon and the family moved to **Greatham**. *When Jack was in his late teens, he had a conversation with his father, during which his father called him 'a chicken' and told him that, "You want to get yourself some of these", pointing to his medals. During the course of the next week, Jack lied about his age and joined the Navy - he wasn't going to have anybody call him a chicken. He told me later in life that the reason he joined the Navy, rather than the Army, was that he didn't want to be "stuck down a foxhole". Jack progressed to being a gun trainer and Navy diver during the war. His most remarkable memory was of serving with the "forgotten fleet" in the Pacific, with the horrific experience of attack by Japanese 'Kamikaze' planes.*

To illustrate the type of man Jack was, one of Jack's shipmates was killed in action. Whilst firing the gun, to try and down the plane before it hit the ship, he had pushed his two colleagues off the gun, forfeiting his own life and saving the life of his mates. Jack saw all this and decided that, when he got back home, he would get in touch with his shipmate's family and tell them how much of a hero he had been. But Jack couldn't find out where they lived after the war. Astonishingly, some sixty years later, he found them living in Oldham in Lancashire. Unbeknown to Jack, his shipmate's wife had a baby boy while they were away, who had never seen his father. Jack was, at last, able to tell his shipmate's son how much of a hero his father was, for which the family was most grateful.

I use this story to illustrate the type of man Jack was - a happy, jolly man, always thinking of other people rather than himself. In fact, he was such a jolly man that, for a good few years, his face was that of the 'Jolly Sailor' pub sign, just outside of Petersfield. I can honestly say that Jack was still cracking his jokes, right up until the end. In the hospital, a very sincere lady doctor looked at Jack and asked, "Is there anything else I can do for you, Mr Dunn?" To which, only Jack could reply, "Yes, what are you doing Monday night?"

Brenda and Jack have had a very happy sixty-two years together, and Nan says she would change absolutely nothing about their years together. I will remember my Grandad as a very happy jolly man, who would do anything for anybody."

After the funeral service, I approached David and made myself known to him. Although living 'up north' himself, he promised me that he would let me have a copy of his tribute in due course – the result of which is shown above. David then told me that his grandfather had been 'something of a poet' and that he would, at some point in the future, like to publish Jack's works, which also included a brief historical account of his own life in the Navy. David must have worked hard on transcribing Jack's written account into computer format, which he would then dispatch to me, part by part, via that wonder of modern science – 'E-mail'. I eventually received this account in full and I am sure Jack would not have minded me doing some editing to turn it into the **'Life of Jack'** book, which I produced on behalf of the Dunn family in 2005.

THE LIFE OF JACK
My early days

My first recollection of life was as a small child, living in Army quarters. My father had come to Longmoor Camp, in Hampshire, to help build the Longmoor Military Railway, sometime in the nineteen-twenties. Dad (Thomas Dunn) had first served with the Lancashire Fusiliers in the Dardanelles

Greatham School as it was when Jack Dunn attended there

during the First World War, where he was injured and presumed dead. Thus it came about that his name appears on the War Memorial up in Salford. So whenever we went to Salford, now part of Greater Manchester, he would proudly show me his name on the Memorial. As he put it, *"He was dead, but he wouldn't lie down"*. When he came back from Gallipoli, he transferred to the Royal Engineers at Catterick Camp (North Yorkshire), where he met my mother, who herself hailed from 'Geordieland', some distance further north.

Mother came from a miner's family of two daughters and five brothers and we used to go up north on visits every Christmas. There were always funerals taking place of men from the local 'pit' – or coalmine. That was a dangerous mine, it was a mile deep and extended some four miles out under the sea. The haulage of the coal tubs was all done by pit ponies. One of my uncles even reckoned he used to drive his ponies in his sleep - the language could be quite educational at times! The miners used to get a coal allowance of about half a ton a month. Young boys used to run after the coal lorry and ask the lady of the house if they could put the load through the hatch. If they had any luck, they would get anything from a threepenny bit to a 'tanner' (sixpence), but that included washing down the cobbles afterwards. The lads sometimes used to run as far as a mile after the lorry to get there first.

It was a hard life those days in Durham. On a Saturday, I used to go to draw my Grandad's pay for his six shifts – for six days a week he used to get just two pounds and six shillings for being a face worker, laid on his side with a huge shovel, loading coal onto a belt. When the Colliery football team was playing, the miners were always very keen to hear the results. So the men working on the cages, sending the tubs down the different seams, used to chalk the score on the side of the tubs. This way the seam workers used to get the score in only a few minutes. Their other favourite sports were 'the greyhounds' and darts. They also had their allotments, where they grew their famous leeks and onions for the local shows. Oh yes, and they were also great pigeon-fanciers.

Anyway, back to Longmoor! When I started my education, it was at the Infants' School, run by the Army, up in the Camp. We had an Army nurse in those days, who used to look after our ailments. The kids used to worship her - indeed, I have seen kids cut themselves so that they could be treated by Sister Phillips. Sadly, she went off on holiday, cut her foot and caught septicaemia, which killed her. All the schoolchildren walked down the road from Longmoor to **Greatham** after the hearse.

Whenever we got any infection as kids, they used to put a notice on your door, *'Keep out – infection'*, while Dad had to go off and sleep in the barracks. We all caught measles so, of course, we had the notice posted on the door. Dad wasn't allowed in the house, but he used to climb through the window and bring us cigarette cards and get his 'NAAFI break'. On one such day, my mother looked out of the window and spotted the Army doctor coming towards our house. She shouted to my Dad, *"Tom, here comes the doctor"*. Dad immediately jumped into the wardrobe and shut the door behind him. My brother and I were laid in bed and in came the doctor to look at us. After checking us over, he then asked, *"How is your Dad?"* My brother then replied, *"You can ask him yourself, he is in the wardrobe"* - and there stood my Dad with his arm slung up at the salute, it was so funny!

My Dad was put on a charge for that and confined to barracks, so we didn't get any fag cards for a week. It's a wonder my brother wasn't strangled! He was the terror of the Camp. He joined the local troop of 'Cubs' and they used to show him how to build a campfire. The following day he built his own campfire on the moors - and burned down over a hundred trees! My Dad was once again on a charge after that escapade. Then, just a week later, the doctor was looking at a child in a pram. My brother had picked up a piece of wood from the NAAFI, with a nail in it, and promptly belted the doctor's backside. The nail sank in and the doctor must have cleared the pram. So poor Dad was placed on a charge yet again. Another week we lost my brother, I think at the time he was only about five years old. They found him walking across the top spar of one of the rail bridges, some thirty feet above the ground. Needless to say, Dad was on yet another charge for that.

I left the Infant School for the older school, which was then being run by Sergeant Faber of the Education Corps, he was a good schoolmaster. An occasion that sticks in my mind was the day that *'HMS Queen Mary'* was launched - that must have been at Southampton. The teacher had the wireless going, so that we could all listen in to the event and, as they broke the cable, I managed to knock a vase of flowers off the table. So, as the *Queen Mary* was launched, I had five whacks across my rear, which certainly made me remember it! My dad sent me down to the stables of the Royal Horse Artillery (RHA) to see Paddy Kennedy for a hair cut. They sat me on a form and give me a cut with the horse shears! When I got home, my mum went spare as I hadn't a hair left on my head. I had to get permission to wear a cap in school.

When we got to the age of ten years, we then had to transfer to **Greatham School** down in the village. I think it was called a Council School in those days, with Mr Charles Wain being the headmaster. Just before that, I'd been a member of the choir at St Martin's Church, which had once been a forage barn for the RHA. The Padre at the time went by the name of Reverend Carter, he was not very well liked by the Army lads. This day in question was very cold and it was very hard to keep warm. So when he got up in the pulpit, he asked if the troops could put *"a little extra"* in the collection bags, to warm the Church. Now it was my job to collect the bags from the soldiers and so, the following Sunday, I went down the aisle with the brass offertory plate to collect the bags. Normally, I could guess by the weight whether we had a good collection or not. This particular week, the bags seemed very light.

My next job was to take the collection into the vestry and count it out into piles of coppers. There was never a lot of silver, as the troops didn't get much a week. *(My own father, with two kids to feed, only got thirty bob a week, that's just £1:50 in today's money.)* When I tipped the bags out I nearly died. To keep the church warm, as requested, they had all brought a small piece of coal each! I just got out quickly, as the Padre went mad. He certainly 'gave them some stick' the following week! I used to go down the NAAFI at the weekend and draw four loaves and a joint of meat for the family. If you gave the Army butcher a 'tip' of sixpence, you usually got a nice joint, but if not, then it was a job to chew it!

Reaching the age of fourteen, I had to leave school and get my first job, which was a paper round, covering the Empshott and Selborne area. I started at 6.30 each morning and usually finished about 1 p.m. The bike I used had no brakes, so it was a wonder I didn't get killed. I stuck to it for just a year,

Brenda Dunn nee Gamblin the girl from Cosham

as I was always getting wet through, while my wage was only fifteen shillings (75p) a week. I then started working for the NAAFI, as errand boy. I used to deliver the paraffin in an old pram, it was a hard job.

(The term 'NAAFI' referred to above stands for Navy, Army and Air Force Institute, an organisation set up for the benefit of the Armed Forces, providing canteen and shopping facilities on a world-wide basis.)

Author's note: All of the above has been extracted from 'The life of Jack', a booklet produced on behalf of the Dunn family. There followed a fascinating account of Jack's Navy service, which is not published here – but the following part of this article describes Jack's return home and subsequent life.

Back home – to a hero's welcome

Heading north, the temperature started dropping, but we were warmed up by the sight of Southsea Castle. We came into Pompey with a 350-foot 'paying-off' pennant streaming out behind us. The then girlfriend – or should I say fiancée? - was on the jetty with my Mum and Dad. The gangway was put down and they all came aboard. My future wife Brenda had got onto the wrong train and had been on the way to Brighton, but she managed to get to the dock with my Mum and Dad in time. They had to come through the hanger, as there were half-naked blokes all over the place, getting ready to go ashore - but nobody seemed to bother.

Lofty was alongside me with his part gammon and he had bought his Mum a set of glamourous black underwear, just like a film star's, which would have fitted a girl of eighteen. His Mum was about sixteen stone and wouldn't have got even one leg into it – but that was Lofty for you! We were then sent to Stamshaw Camp, Cosham, and two days later we were demobbed. I dropped the outfitter ten bob (fifty pence in today's money!) and he fitted me up with a nice clerical grey suit, shirt and raincoat, shinny shoes and a pork pie hat. It was the first suit I had ever owned. Then it was off home with Mum, Dad and Bren.

I arrived at Liss Station, having been away for some two years, when a chap called Fred Watts, who was in the Liss Fire Brigade, spotted me and shouted, *"Home again then, Jack?"* I could have choked him, as I'd been away for two years and he'd never even been out of Liss – still, that's life. Then it was on the *Liss & District* bus to **Greatham** and home, where the banners were out – *"Welcome home"* - it was all a bit embarrassing.

My Dad asked me, *"How did you get on son?"* I thought I would put one over on him, knowing that he had once served in Egypt. I told him that I had to patrol the brothels in 'Alex' and, on checking one of them, I told him that the old Madam who ran the place asked me where I came from. I told her that I was from England and that my father had served in Egypt many years ago. She then said, *"I knew an English soldier that was in the REs, his name was Tommy Dunn"*. The look on my Dad's face was one of shock, but his instant reply was, *"Don't go telling your mother about this"*. He must have known I was only leg pulling.

The final crack was that I got my medals, two more than Dad, but he told me that I'd earned mine! I answered, *"Where do you think I got them from, off a Colman's mustard tin?"* He was really proud of me, but I had to have my joke, I had waited a long time. But after all we went through it still makes you wonder who won the bloody war, there is still fighting all over the world. So there I was, signing off, with no hammock to sling and back to civvie-street and a demob suit. Before I had gone into the Navy, I had joined the Home Guard at the tender age of sixteen. I was provided with a broom handle with a bayonet tied on one end and told that if a paratrooper came down, I was to run out and hold the bayonet under his backside! Why should Britain tremble, eh?

Looking back now, I was lucky to get home after some near misses. My worst time was when I fell off the bottom of the old ship, while cleaning an inlet valve. They say that if you drop more than thirty feet, your body is pushed up into your helmet! I hit the bottom of Sydney Harbour, which thankfully was only ten feet from the bottom of the ship. Your life certainly flashes before you in a second at times like that. But I have never regretted volunteering, you don't know how ignorant you are about how the rest of the world survives. You go to war as a boy and come back a man.

Civvie Street

I had a week's holiday and then realised that I had to earn my keep. So I went back to my old firm, driving heavy lorries, luckily they took me on straight away. But the trucks were in a hell of a state, as any good motor at the start of the war had been taken over by the Army. The brakes weren't all that good so I used to put my trust in the Lord and keep my bowels open. I was still courting Bren and eventually, in 1947, I asked her if she could put up with me for life. She said *"Yes"*, she must have thought I had money, Ha-ha, joke!

We were married at Wymering Church and it was definitely the best move I ever made. It has now lasted nearly sixty years, we have two great kids, with grandchildren and great-grandchildren. We tied the knot in the month of March, so we got a bit of tax back, the grand sum of £24. We were actually married on a total of seventy quid, my reward for serving King and country. Life was pretty hard, but we managed to get a two-up and two-down cottage, no drains and no sanitation. I had spent most of my life in Army quarters, so I wasn't used to having a bucket to empty every week and nor was Bren. Then it started getting really modern - they sent a lorry around to empty the bucket. You can't stop progress! Ha-ha! I will now sign off, as Sunday dinner has arrived!

From an old ex-matelot, PJX 298263.

(Jack Dunn wrote the final words above on the Sunday before he was taken into hospital. Brenda later told me that she swears Jack had a premonition that those words would be his last attempt at writing. Ed.)

Life in post-war Greatham

Everyone in those days was on rations - food, blankets and furniture. Our bedside cabinets were just orange boxes with curtains across them. The house was so very cold in the winter, we even used to put the carpet on the bed as well. I remember that one night the bed went down at one end. We had gone through the worm-eaten floor and the legs were sticking through the kitchen ceiling. If you had the money, you could buy those items you needed, as most things were issued on dockets. In 1947, my wage was £3 and ten shillings a week. We didn't get much meat a week, so Bren used to give me extra potatoes and veg to fill me up. I used to carry a pellet gun with me on the lorry - I will admit that I was something of a poacher, but only to help out with the food shortage.

The village rumour mongers all thought we'd had to get married, but they had to wait another two years before we had our daughter Jennifer. When she started teething, it was hell, she would cry all night. I used to go to work in a dream. I used to pick Bren up in the lorry, along with Jennifer, and she used to sleep all day with the motion – but then howl all night. My lorry was pretty rough though, as at times you could not stop very quickly when fully loaded. I told Bren *"If I say jump - jump!"* It certainly taught you how to drive! Two years later we had John, who was totally different - he would sleep all through the night.

We had many amusing situations at work. One of our drivers, George Webb, had just come out of the RAF, so he used to wear his old battle dress for work. One job was to take lime to this chicken farm and spread it in the chicken runs, to sweeten the ground. We took the sheet off the load and hung it over the wire netting. Inside the run were several sheep and a ram, which kept butting the folded sheet. I said to George that rams were allergic to the colour blue. So if he put his behind to the wire netting, the ram would back away. He said, *"You're pulling my leg!"* I told him, *"Okay then, try it and I'll prove it is true"*.

George put his rear end to the wire, then looked back and saw the ram backing away. I started to speak to George and, of course, he looked back at me. At that point the ram put his head down and charged. It hit George dead on target, knocking him straight across the road, and he hit the chicken run opposite. The wire bent over and then flicked back up, George did a complete somersault into the muck run. He got up and then chased me round the chicken farm with his shovel. I am sure he would have crowned me if he'd caught me, Ha-ha. Even now, at over ninety years of age, old George still has a laugh about it.

We were then given some German POWs to help us, some were from the *'Volksturm'*, their Home Guard. I remember that one of them was only four foot six. They were great lads, they hadn't wanted to fight any more than we did, and it turned out that they were very good workers. Another time, I had a Romany lad called Jim as a driver's mate. He used to back up the lorry under a big chute to load up with lime. Sometimes, the live lime used to stick in the chute, so he had to go up and poke the lime to start it flowing again. All of a sudden, there was a hell of a rush of lime and he came through the chute as well.

Brenda and Jack married at Wymering March 1947

I filled the lorry dead level in about two seconds, when up through the lime appeared Jim, still with his trilby on and looking like *'Snow White'*. His eyes, ears and nose were full of lime. I lifted him off and washed him off in a rainwater tank, he was really shook up. But it had been a comical sight to see him rising to the surface through the lime!

I had another mate, who we called 'Yorkie', his surname was Spenceley. He was very fond of sparring about, flicking your nose with his hand. But on this particular day, as he put out his arm, I snatched him to my chest. Now, I'm fifty-odd inches around the chest and I have always been strong in the arms, so as I gave him a squeeze, he went out like a light. I had scary visions of the noose, hanging on the end of its rope - I thought I had killed him. I managed to get some water out of a ditch and bathed his face. It took twenty minutes to bring him round, but he didn't spar any more after that.

As mentioned previously, those lorries were in a hell of a state. One I had the misfortune to drive literally used to drink oil. There was a long slope from Midhurst up to Redford and, when we were fully loaded, my young mate used to stand on the front bumper and pour a gallon of oil into the engine while we were still under way. You couldn't do that nowadays, with all the traffic. In fact, the wagons wouldn't even be on the road today, with the MoT regulations. There was one day, when I was going down a country lane loaded with lime, that I came to a hairpin bend with a farmyard right on the corner. The steering went completely and I ran into the five-barred gate head on. The gate flew open and I hit a very large heap of cow manure, about thirty or forty tons of it. The stuff went in all directions and drove the engine back into the cab. I shot forward into the windscreen, but got away with just a bump. That was the end of that old heap.

Another job I had to do was to take one of those old 1928 bull-nosed *Morris* vans to *Smiths'* clock factory, to deliver a load of electric coils. There was no foot brake at all and only the merest fraction of a handbrake. I would put the seat as close as I could to the steering wheel so that, when I went across London, I would have one hand on the handbrake, signal with my right arm and steer a straight line with my stomach - it was certainly an adventure! You'd never do it nowadays, the way the traffic is.

Working at Longmoor Camp

Eventually, the transport business got a bit dodgy, so I got a job in the Longmoor Garrison Engineers' yard, doing maintenance on the married quarters and the Army Camp. I had a year during which I worked on plumbing, but then they ran short of money and, instead, I then got a job at the NAAFI store and shop. Mr Seaton was the manager and I got made up to charge-hand. We used to supply the local units with their rations, as well as all the Officers' and Sergeants' Messes. We had one officers' wife who had been in India for many years. She would try and knock you down on the price of the fruit, as she used to make a lot of jam. When I used to see her coming, I would put up the price of the plums by tuppence (two old pennies) a pound. I would then tell her that, if she took seven pounds at a time, I would take tuppence a pound off. I would win every time, Ha-ha.

If one of the girls served her (it was all counter service in those days), then she would ask for half-a-pound of *Rover* assorted biscuits. The girl would give her a half-pound packet but she would refuse them, saying that she wanted loose biscuits. She would then add, *"Jack knows what I have"*. They used to shout at me to come into the shop. I would see her and say, *"Good morning Mrs McDonald, you want your usual biscuits?" "Yes please, Jack"*, she'd reply. I would then go out into the back, undo a packet of *Rover*, and pour them into a bag. Then I'd march back into the shop and weigh them up, chip in with a *"Thank you madam"*, and off she'd go, as happy as Larry! She'd occasionally ask me *"Why don't the girls serve me loose ones?"* but my reply means that I'll never go to heaven.

We used to get the Army Reserves every

year for a fortnight's camp. They used to put officers in charge of the Mess, but they didn't know very much about the job, so we used to help them a lot, especially when the GOC's visit was due – that's the General Officer Commanding. One young officer came down in a panic, so it was a case of *"Jack, can you help?"* He had forgotten the flowers for the centre of the table and was terrified. I told him not to worry, then went home and picked a load of dahlia heads. We had no vases, so I told him to put the heads down the centre of the table, at which he asked, *"Are you sure?"* But he did as he was told and earned himself a hell of a pat on the back from the General!

One officer used to ask for things that he thought I knew nothing about. I overheard him tell his subaltern that he wanted some *Port Salut* cheese served at the next function. I quickly got my book out, before he came in, the bigheaded sod. He said to me, *"I don't suppose you know what Port Salut cheese is, do you Jack?"* to which I replied, *"Oh yes. It's a special cheese made by Trappist Monks in Northern France"*. He was amazed at that, while the young subaltern was tickled to death, he used to laugh every time he came in. The bumptious officer never tried it again after that.

Another laugh came when I used to go around the officers' married quarters to take their orders. Major Higgins' wife used to say, *"Come in Jack, I'm in bed, just come up!"* It was a bit embarrassing, she had no shame, and I had to tell myself, *"You are a married man, Jack"*. Talk about opportunity knocks! A few days later, she came into the shop and the manager mentioned that her monthly account was overdue. She turned around to me and said. *"Jack, are you going around with the order?"* *"Yes"*, I replied. To which she then said, *"Well, will you go upstairs in my house and get my cheque book. It's near where you normally sit when you take my order"*. Was I blushing! The manager asked, *"What the hell do you get up to?"* but he knew what she was like.

Another officer's wife used to come in and ask one of the girls for bacon. The girl would weigh it up and then the lady would then say, *"That's not my usual bacon, get Jack, he knows"*. So I used to take the bacon out the back, turn it over on the greaseproof paper, then go back into the shop and show it to the lady in question. She would then remark, *"Why can't that girl serve me like that?"* Then she'd head off home happy.

Becoming a butcher

I then changed jobs, going to work as a butcher at Bordon. What a job that was, from 5.30 in the morning until 6 o'clock at night, with deliveries to be made all around the camp. But there were quite a few laughs on that job too. I delivered a chicken to one Army quarter and the lady who answered the door was very attractive, standing there in a flesh-coloured bikini. I was quite taken aback, as she was blonde and just like a *'Page Three'* girl. Now when I used to take their orders, I would ask if they wanted sage and onion stuffing. If they said, *"Yes please"*, I would write 'S/O' on their order. But now, with the shock of seeing her state of dress, I forgot all about the stuffing.

I'd just got back to my van when a load of Army lads went doubling past on PT. Our pin-up came out into the rain in her bikini and shouted across, *"Jack, I wanted stuffing as well!"* Oh my god, for the next six months, wherever I was, all around the Camp, any lads on PT used to shout, *"Hey butcher, we want stuffing"*. She probably didn't realise what she had said at the time, but she also pulled my leg for weeks afterwards.

I also used to deliver to the caravan site, where this one woman had ordered pig's liver. I knocked at the door and a voice said, *"Come in"*. What a shock! I went into the van and she was stood there, stark naked, in the bath. I twisted around to leave and found that my fifty-odd inch chest was jammed in the caravan doors, which were very narrow. I struggled through and literally fell out into a bed of flowers, with the liver sliding all over me. What a life!

After ten years in that job, the Bordon butcher sold up, so I went to work for the *Gateways Supermarket* down in Petersfield. That was another place for laughs. One lady was the widow of a Naval Commander, who had gone down with his ship. I used to bring up things in conversation to try and cheer her up. This one time I mentioned that it was quite a feat to bring up the *'Mary Rose'*. (That was the flagship of King Henry VIII, which sank in 1545, then raised from the seabed of the Solent off Southsea in 1982. Personally, I thought it was a waste of money.) Her next comment was, *"Butcher, were you on the 'Mary Rose'?"* My young butcher's boy laughed his head off. I replied, *"Madam, I wasn't very familiar with Henry the Eighth!"* She then thought about it for a minute and asked, *"I suppose that is what they call a Navy clanger?"* It was several months before that topic died down.

Another good laugh - a lady used to come in that owned *'Tiger Toys'*. She never liked waiting. She was on the bacon counter one day and I was serving about six people on the butchery. She shouted across, *"Butcher, have you got chicken legs?"* I couldn't resist the swift riposte, *"Madam, my legs have gone that shape running backwards and forwards behind this block"*. She never came in any more, thank goodness. One day, I was trying to deal with half a dozen people waiting to be served, when Bren came into the shop, marched up to the front of the queue and asked me what time I'd be home. One lady customer said, *"Take your turn"*, even though Bren had only asked a question. Being a leg-puller, I just said to the lady, *"It's OK madam, it's just the woman I sleep with"*.

She never cottoned on for about six months that it was a wind-up, she continued to give my wife dirty looks.

At that time we had a meat supervisor who had no time for older butchers. He came in one day, bragging that he had just got rid of a butchery manager of sixty years old. Not long after that, he started on me. I got so wound up that I chucked in the manager's job and got transferred to the Liphook branch, where I worked right up until I was sixty-eight. They gave me a great send off when I finally retired, about fifty of my old bosses and staff. So both Bren and I now work in a Charity shop for half a day each week. It's great seeing a lot of my old customers, apart from picking up a lot of bargains.

I really think we should get a Red Cross for my car, as I regularly visit an old Navy chum who is very ill with angina and stone trouble. Another chum of mine is dying of cancer - I supply him every week with videos. Yet another old pal suffers with severe depression, another one has had a bad heart attack, while an old mate of ninety years old has just gone into a home.

I still dress up as Father Xmas every year for the Bordon children, then for the local old peoples' home. Another two days I entertain for the kindergarten up at the School. There are so many tasks I do over two days, such as Saturday for the Heart Foundation Xmas Party and Sunday it's the Xmas dinner at the *'Country Market'* complex up at Bordon.

Peter Gripton

Chpater 15
Pilgrims Way (formerly Robins)

*(Following the article that I was able to put together in reference to Keeper's Cottage, I sent off two of my history books to ladies who had once lived in **Greatham** many years previously. The first was to Prue Swatton, now resident in Bath, Somerset and the second to her cousin, Caroline Blackwell, who now lives in Suffolk. Caroline – who is better known to her family and friends as Betty – was kind enough to add her own memories of living here in Hampshire and they appear below. Ed.)*

Betty's mother, Martha Elizabeth (but always called Pat by her family), was one of the four children born to Thomas and Caroline Corps (pronounced *Core*), who once lived at Keeper's Cottage, towards the bottom end of Church Lane, **Greatham**, until later moving to Robins Cottage, just a short distance away. *(That must have been when the Lacey family left, moving to Gould's House, around 1931. Ed.)* Pat was the youngest child of the Corp family, her three elder brothers being Walter, William and Thomas. *(The Corps family is shown in a photograph, taken outside Keeper's Cottage in about 1901.)*

Betty has no memories herself of Keeper's Cottage, but was told many stories of her family's life there. Gran (Caroline) would often walk as far as Liss to do her shopping and, more often than not, she would be pushing along a pram in front of her! She used to sit up late at night making shirts for her three sons. Nothing was wasted in those days; even old huntsmen's coats would be cut up and sewn onto backing material to make rugs for the floor. Today this would be called recycling! Any tramp or vagrant that turned up at the door – and there were quite a few back then – would be offered the use of a bowl of water and a towel in order that they could wash their aching feet, something that they much appreciated. Gran once caught one of the soldiers from nearby Longmoor Camp 'raiding' her crop of apples and smilingly rebuked him by telling him, *"If you had asked me, Tommy, I would have given you some apples"*. Betty recalls her Gran as a very gentle lady, who would never raise her voice, whatever the perceived provocation.

Betty's mother had happy memories of hop picking locally, when whole families would often spend their working days in the open air – the only drawback being the scratches regularly received from the hop-bines. A 'tally-man' would keep a record of how much each family had picked and Gran would gratefully put away the money earned, to pay for the next winter's coal supply. Betty remembers her mother telling her that, if ever she had toothache, she would take a bucket of ice-cold water to the end of the garden and dip her face into it. This would help in relieving the pain - and also prevent Gran from worrying! The nearest dentist could possibly have been at Liss, or even as far as Petersfield, so self-help obviously became order of the day.

East-enders

Betty was born in 1929 and has fond memories of spending several childhood holidays, along with her mother, at her grandparents' home at Robins, probably between the years 1932 and 1937. It was a totally different world from the one where she was then living, at Leytonstone, in the 'East End' of London. With the cottage being surrounded by fields, she recalls having to walk through herds of cows as a regular occurrence. Once, when walking through a field with her mother, they found a pony amongst the cows. Mother explained to her that it had once belonged to a circus and had been trained to put its head between the clowns' legs and tip them over. Needless to say, Betty made sure that she steered clear of the pony!

She can remember walking around on his 'morning rounds' with her Granddad, who would allow her to place sprigs of his home grown parsley at the top of the rabbit warrens, to tempt out the rabbits for a snack. This she did – but cannot recall seeing any rabbits feasting! Granddad himself didn't set out to catch any rabbits, but there were a few local men who used to place nets across these warrens, then send in their ferrets to chase the rabbits out from the other end.

Betty also remembers Granddad opening the gate to one field, in order that the local hunt could pass through into Church Lane, possibly on its way back to the Manor House. Granddad was one of many local people employed by the Harrisons of Le Court and Betty says that she was always told that they were lovely people to work for. *(Sir Heath Harrison died in 1934 and Lady Harrison in 1938. Ed.)* At the end of each working day, the old man would bring home a pail full of lovely fresh creamy milk straight from the cowsheds – no need for pasteurisation in those days!

For home lighting at Robins, a huge old oil lamp was employed, but Betty remembers being taken to bed by candlelight. Once, her Gran held the candle too close to herself and singed her hair, which frightened poor Betty! The other thing that usually made her feel scared was when the bats would swoop around her in the garden at dusk. A frequent visitor for Betty's Gran was the old gentleman who lived further up Church Lane, she thinks his name was Eli Toll. He was virtually blind and would have to feel his way around the table before shaking hands with Gran.

Members of the Corps family at Robins Cottage in 1935

Betty can just about recall attending the village school at times, and also 'Sunday school' up at the Church. She fondly remembers the lych gate, although at the time she hadn't realised that it was the Harrisons who had presented it to the village. In the family circle, the name of Captain Coryton was often mentioned, although Betty was too small then to remember in what context. She says that the main things she remembers about walking up the lane was that it often used to flood, so that her mother had to pick her up and carry her; then there was the raucous sound made by the rooks, nesting high in the trees above the lane.

It must have been to 'Nanny' Russell's 'sweet shop' in Swain's Cottage that Betty went for her occasional treat. On one occasion, a gypsy child came in at the same time, trampling all over Betty's feet in her eagerness to get to the counter. Betty was not impressed with the girl's manners, or by the lack of apology for her rude behaviour. Another occasional highlight was to drop in on Mr Shepherd, the village blacksmith, along the Selborne road. Betty would watch in fascination, looking over the half-door of the forge, as this hard-working artisan pumped the bellows and heated the horseshoes in the red-hot coals. She was amazed at the patience of the horses as they stood waiting – and then didn't even flinch when the hot shoes were nailed onto their hooves. *(The aptly named Forge House now occupies the site of the original blacksmith's shop. Ed.)*

Happy memories

Betty still looks back on her childhood years at **Greatham** with great affection. One of her fondest memories is of sitting one day with her Aunt Florence (Prue's mother) in the garden outside Robins, where she was encouraged to learn the Ten Commandments, in two consecutive sessions of five at a time. *"What would you like, a penny or a kiss?"* her Aunt asked, when the first five had been memorised and correctly presented. Being tactful, Betty replied that she preferred 'the kiss', knowing that she would inevitably get 'the penny' after reciting the second five!

Eventually, Betty's grandparents had to leave Robins and they went to stay with Betty's family in Essex. It must have been quite difficult for them, to adjust from their country cottage to the bustle of town. But Betty recalls her Gran saying how nice it was to have instant hot and cold water at the turn of a tap – something she had never previously experienced whilst at **Greatham**.

Betty now lives in Clare, a small village, this time in the lovely surroundings of Suffolk. Close by is another village called Cavendish, where by coincidence Lady Sue Ryder had her headquarters. In fact Betty and her husband used to help in the office and often met up with the great Leonard Cheshire. They well remember his deep and unusual voice. This has reinforced Betty's special interest in the very first Cheshire Home at **Greatham**, as the Le Court estate was the very place at which her grandfather had once worked.

Having read **'A History of Greatham'**, Betty finds it hard to believe that there was a **Greatham** that existed outside the confinement of Church Lane; most of her memories are of that small area that lies between Robins and the Church. She also wishes that her mother could have read the book, it would have revived so many special memories for her too. She adds that it would be a joy to visit **Greatham** once more, but with advancement of years it is proving to be only a dream.

Footnote

Betty was kind enough to send the following poem, *'Those Latin Names'*, which is obviously a favourite of hers:

*It was a simple country child
Who took me by the hand;
Why English flowers had Latin names,
She could not understand.
Those funny, friendly English flowers
That bloom from year to year;
She asked me if I would explain
And so I said to her:*

*"Eranthus is an aconite,
As everybody knows,
And Helleborus Niger is
Our friend the Christmas rose.
Galanthus is a snowdrop,
Matthiola is a stock
And Cardamine's the meadow flower,
Which you call lady's smock.
Muscari is grape hyacinth,
Dianthus is a pink –
And that's as much as one small head
Can carry, I should think."*

*She listened very patiently
Then turned, when I had done,
To where a fine Forsythia
Was smiling in the sun.
Said she, "I love this yellow stuff",
And that, somehow, seemed praise enough.*

Reginald Arkell

Chapter 16
The Shotter Family

My book *'A History of Greatham'* included a complete chapter referring to the Shotter family, who once lived at Deal Farm. Dr Ronald Shotter, who now lives in Croydon, south London, provided the bulk of what is contained in that chapter. He recently sent me copies of two census forms, from 1891 and 1901, on which the names of his ancestors are shown as living in **Greatham**. In 1891, the address was written as 'Church Lane Cottage, 2 Tenement', while in 1901 this had altered slightly to 'Old Church Lane Cottages (1). This would now be 'Swain's Cottage', which includes all previous properties.

The inhabitants listed in 1891 are as follows:

William Shotter, head of family, aged 33, farm labourer, born **Greatham**

Sarah, his wife, also aged 35, from Kingsbury, Middlesex

James, their son, aged 12, is termed 'odd boy on farm'

The other children are Priscilla, George, Gowan, William and John, all shown as born here in **Greatham**.

By 1901, the census return shows the following:

William, head of family, now aged 43 and described as 'Stockman on farm'

Sarah, his wife, now aged 45

George, their son, now aged 18 and a 'Bricklayer's labourer'

William, another son, aged 13, shown as an 'Under-gardener (domestic)'

Son John is by now aged 11 and there are two further children, Sarah and Elizabeth.

Another daughter, Emily, was born just two years after that 1901 census, and was the aunt of Ronald. Some of the names provided by Ron in the book are not shown on the census forms, for one reason or another, but those that do appear certainly tie in with the wonderful story that he originally provided.

The large Shotter family at Deal Farm

Chapter 17
Winifred Murphy (1906-2004)

At the July 2002 meeting of **Greatham** Women's Institute (WI), Mrs Winifred Murphy (nee Farr) almost certainly created a national WI record, because that meeting celebrated eighty years of unbroken membership. Win, as she was affectionately known to one and all, joined the WI at Rowledge (near Farnham, Surrey) on July 16th 1922. It was her 16th birthday, the youngest age then at which girls could become members. Since those early days, Win has regularly attended meetings and has held just about every possible role within the groups with which she has served.

On the celebratory afternoon, Win was smartly dressed in a white sweatshirt, bearing both the old and new badges of the WI organisation. In her inimitable manner, Win also made all the sandwiches and supplied all the biscuits for the customary 'tea', after the meeting in **Greatham** Village Hall. The tea was supplemented by a rich fruit cake, decorated in the WI colours and bearing matching decorative ribbons. A card from the Hampshire Federation of WI, congratulating her on her eighty years of membership, was proudly displayed alongside the cake.

As a young girl, Win Farr attended Farnham Girl's Grammar School, in the days when it operated from West Street. From her desk, she was the first person to see the Union Flag, hoisted upon the Post Office building opposite, in recognition of the signing of the Armistice that ended the First World War. Win worked for both The Weavers, in Lion and Lamb Yard, and J. Smyth's in East Street, prior to her marriage; after it, she carried out *"duties of national importance"* during World War II.

Right up until her death, early this year, Win remained remarkably upright and active at her home in Wesley Lodge on Longmoor Road. She still carried out as much of her own cooking and cleaning as possible. Win purchased her own copy of *'A History of Greatham'* and, just prior to her death, asked me to take her a copy that she wished to present to Shirley Farrar who had lived next door and who had always *been "a good and kind neighbour"*.

*Win Murphy, stalwart of the **Greatham** branch of the Women's Institute*

Chapter 18
The Foster Connection

On January 6th 2005, I received an e-mail that read as follows:

*"I have a very old letter (1805 or 1808) which discusses the history of the (old) church and the village. If you would like a copy, please let me know your address. (My great grandfather was Joseph Foster, Rector of **Greatham**.)*

Regards, Nigel Foster"

My interest was immediately aroused by this message and I made contact with Nigel to confirm my interest in 'the letter'. By the next morning, a copy of the letter had already arrived through the post, and I have pleasure in reproducing the text below.

From 'The Gentleman's Magazine'

Havant, January 14 1805

Mr Urban,

*To assist a Reverend and Learned writer with some Materials for the projected 'History of the Antiquities of Hampshire', should his intention be revived, I have sent you a few notes respecting **Greatham** for insertion in your Magazine.*

*Before the Conquest, the **Manor of Greatham** was part of the possession of Queen Edda (Edith). At the general survey, the woods there furnished sustenance for thirty hogs; and Waleran the Hunter possessed one hide of land.*

The Manor Farm had formerly an admitted claim of turning all livestock on Woolmere Forest at proper seasons, except sheep; for, being close grazers, they would pick out the finest grasses and hinder the deer from thriving; for this privilege, the owner payed (sic) the King annually a bushel of oats.

The Manor is now the property of Francis Love Beckford Esq.; the Manor House and demense lands called Le Court having been sold off from the Manor in 1577 to Mr Lewkner.

The Church appears to have been erected about the 15th-century and consists of a single nave, with a chancel extending beyond it. The simplicity of the building attracts our notice and much may be said in favour of its sequestered situation, in the middle of the village. On entering the Porch, we perceive the following grotesque declaration, in large letters over the door:

"Avoid profane man, curse not here;

None but the holy, pure and clere

As he that goeth to be so,

Into this porch but further go."

Adjoining to the pulpit against the south wall is placed a sumptuous tomb, with the following inscription: *

"To the Memorie of Dame Marjorie Caryll who, having sure confidence in the merits of our Saviour, Jesus Christ, departed this life with great courage and comfort the 11th daie of Maie, Anno Domini 1632, in the 40th yeere of her age. This vertuous ladie was the wife of Sir Richard Caryll of Harting, Knight, with whom she lived seven yeeres and, after his death, continued his widowe all the time of her life, being the space of sixteen yeeres."

"Thou marble tumbe though long ye mayst endure

And dost within an honord corps immure,

Yet raised and freed thy prisonr God

shall see

When thou forever shallt demolishd bee.

A jewell then of price thou dost containe,

Which thou consumed, for ever shalt remaine."

Johannes Love cognatus devotissimus.

(* *Readers of my book* 'A History of Greatham' *will recognise the above quotations, which appear on page 26. Some of the spelling in the letter differs from that in my own reading, but nevertheless confirms that a time span of 200 years does not alter the meaning! Ed.)*

On the opposite side is the following inscription, to the memory of a pious and excellent Clergyman, who always proved himself sincere in the cause of Religion and warm with sentiments of humanity.

(There then follow the words devoted to the Rev Richard Newlin, which I will not repeat here, but which can be found on page 27 of the history book. Ed.)

The large yew tree in the churchyard extends its sable branches over the mouldering graves and, having withstood several ages, remains a pleasing monument of ascetic and equity.

Rectors: Edmund (or Edward?) Golden, in 1728

Richard Newlin, died 1772

Edmund (or Edward?) White, present Rector

Greatham is valued in the King's books at £6. 5s. 10d. Yearly tithes 12s. 7d. and dedicated to St John the Baptist.

Father Paul

Foster family tree

(When I was researching the history book, someone must have passed on to me a copy of the Foster family tree. Having again looked through my archive material, I saw that the names Nigel and Alex were appended in manuscript at the very bottom of the tree.

Most interesting though is the fact that the family can trace its blood line directly back to King Edward I, who reigned as King of England from 1274 to 1307. Joseph Foster, mentioned by Nigel in my opening paragraph, was Rector of **Greatham** *1879 - 80, although he had previously been Curate-in-charge from 1866 to 1875. Foster family members, then resident at Le Court, were the main benefactors for the gift of land for the present-day Church, whose construction was completed in 1875. Ed.)*

A short while after having made contact with Nigel Foster, he was kind enough to send me a copy of the original research that had been carried out in reference to the 'Family Tree'. That research was apparently done by Joseph Foster and is designated with the place and date of *"New Barnet, Herts, 1871"*. Joseph introduced his paper as follows:

"When I began to collect the materials for a Second Edition of the Forster Pedigree, I did not anticipate the results which this volume presents. And yet it has been impossible, in the time taken to compile this edition, to give anything approaching to a complete Pedigree, as the family is, and has been, much more numerous than would be generally supposed. However, should a Third Edition be called for in the course of another decade, I hope I shall then be able to give as comprehensive an account as the materials at hand will furnish."

It is of interest to note that the family name 'Foster' had been derived from the original one of 'Forster'. One branch of this "ancient and numerous family" was descended from the first upon record, one "Gilbert de Buckton, also called Gilbert Forster, alias Forrester, Chief Gamekeeper to the Bishop of Durham, living in the time of King John and King Henry III", who died in 1342. Buckton was described as "a hamlet in the chapelry of Kyloe, in the parish of Holy Island".

Family records indicate that Joseph Foster, the gentleman concerned so much with **Greatham** and its ministry, was born at Fakenham, Norfolk, on December 9th 1834; he married Letitia Frances Philpot at Lydney, Gloucestershire, on May 15th 1862. An older brother, also named Joseph, had also been born at Fakenham on February 24th 1833, but died less than a year later, on February 6th 1834. Going back much further in time, the first mention of this branch of the family would seem to be one Robert Forster, *"to whom his father gave lands in Cold Hesledon, County Durham, in the time of Henry VII"*.

Accompanying the 'family tree' material was the will of Sampson Foster (dated 1869), with an added codicil dated 1870. In it, the said gentleman was described as *"formerly of the City of Norwich and Squire of Stamford Hill in the County of Middlesex, but now of Le Court in the County of Hampshire"*. Sampson Foster appointed his three sons, William Fry Foster, Sampson Lloyd Foster and the Reverend Joseph Foster, to be trustees and executors of his will.

Chapter 19
Greatham Allotments

Allotment gardens have long been a familiar sight in the towns, cities and villages around the country. Many of them now belong to the community and are administered by local Councils, committees, gardening clubs and horticultural societies. It is probably many years since **Greatham** had any official tending of such allotments, but documents recently brought to light show that the pastime was very popular during the last century. In 1924, for instance, the Coryton family 'allotted' areas of land for local villagers, in plots measured in the old method of 'roods'. Two separate areas were indicated, one designated as 'Church Field', alongside the 'high road to Hawkley' and the second at Ham Barn.

The names of the villagers who subscribed to the upkeep of the allotments, then owned by A F Coryton at Manor House, are shown below. They make up a cross-section of the inhabitants of those far-off days of the 'Roaring Twenties', just after the First World War and before the troubled economic times of the Thirties.

Church Field Allotments

Plot 1.	G. Mitchell
Plot 2.	W. Knight
Plot 3.	E. Vidler
Plot 4.	F. Aburrow
Plot 5.	G. Clarke
Plot 6.	H. Fisher
Plot 7.	G. Howard
Plot 8.	G. Laker
Plot 9.	F. Edwards
Plot 10.	R. Edwards
Plot 11.	F. Mells (Mrs)
Plot 12.	T. Clear
Plot 13.	D. Rasell
Plot 14.	G. Macey
Plot 15.	A. Cornwall
Plot 16a.	G. Laker
Plot 16b.	E. Knowles
Plot 17a.	A. W. Binagay
Plot 17b.	C. H. Hewlett
Plot 18a.	F. Bicknell
Plot 18b.	J. Oliver
Plot 19.	S. Albery
Plot 20a.	B. Pullinger
Plot 20b.	W. Alford
Plot 21a.	W. Knowles
Plot 21b.	E. Penfold
Plot 22a.	R. Howard
Plot 22b.	C. H. Hewlett
Plot 23.	? Whittington

Ham Barn Allotments

Plot 1a.	W. Davey
Plot 2.	J. Symons
Plot 3.	M. Tigg
Plot 4.	T. Seaward
Plot 5.	G. Saunders
Plot 5a.	T. Swyers
Plot 6.	G. Lodge
Plot 6.a.	E. Austin

History

Early in 2006, the Parish Magazine brought to light a 'potted history' of the Allotment Charity, in an article written by the incumbent Chairman of the Trustees, Roger Lewis, living in Todmore, the location for the garage that used to occupy that space. The land for the allotments was situated between **Greatham** and Selborne, to the left of the main road going away from the village, just before reaching Le Court. It had been bequeathed to **Greatham** at the end of

1851, for use by poor people of the parish. In accordance with the 1848 Charity Act, a charity was formed and trustees appointed.

Following parish boundary changes in 1928, the trustees found this quite a problem, as the charitable deed clearly designated the old original boundaries of the allotment. In 1952 the four acres of land had been rented out for grazing and, in August 1969, the old charitable deed had disappeared. At this stage, the Charity Commission now issued a new deed but, apart from the land and its rent, the charity found itself with little or no funding.

In 2001 the tenant died and the trustees decided that the land should be sold. The problem here was that the land hadn't been registered, so title had to be established. After frustrating delays in resolving this problem, the land was finally sold off in December 2003. Amazingly, despite there now being no land or allotments, the charity still exists and is presently trying to redefine the purpose of the charity and how to use any remaining funds.

Chapter 20
Greatham Service Station

It was Mr Frank Madgwick who built the garage on Petersfield Road, around 1947, and Mrs Madgwick continued living nearby right up until her death. The site had originally been used as a builder's yard by W A Kemp and Sons, as can be seen in a photograph of the time. It must have been an ideal location for a garage in those days, when the main A325 road ran through the middle of the village. By 1963, the garage was still called **Greatham Motors**, becoming **Greatham Service Station** in 1964, when it was taken over by Ray Flack. Apart from serving *National Benzol* petrol, it offered car sales, hire purchase, MoTs, repairs, a break-down service and car insurance.

There was a café on the site, which became very popular with the local youngsters, with a jukebox playing out the songs of the day. Almost everyone locally used the service station, and, on Saturday mornings, it was quite the local community centre. Locally based soldiers, no doubt from both Longmoor and Bordon, came in on their Wednesday afternoon 'sports day' and the garage was kept open overnight a couple of times a year, to look after motorbike riders having a rally on nearby Weaver's Down. The café was demolished around 1973, after the law decided it wouldn't allow 'peg boarding' on the walls - or the whole building being supported on 5-gallon oil-drums filled with sand! Anther factor in its demise must have been that café customers had to share toilet facilities with the garage staff.

Motor marques sold at the garage included *Ford*, *Rootes*, *Chrysler*, *Hillman*, (remember the *Allegro* and *Imp*?) and *Skoda*, while another service was provided by *Berri Motors Van Hire*. Brands of fuel included *National Benzol*, *Regent* and *Premium*. It

Kemp's builders site. alongside Elm Villa (now Chalfont)

Pat and Ray's first home in the village

also became the first service station in the country to be owned by *ARCO (Atlantic Richfield)*, but as they didn't have their own signs available, fuel was sold under the sign *'Quality Petrol'*.

The workshop became well known over a wide area, for being able to tackle the simplest job, right up to the most complicated – in fact there weren't many problems that could not be solved. At this time, the garage was open from 7.30am to 9pm on Monday to Saturday and 10am to 4pm on Sunday. There were no self-service pumps, attendants actually came out from a small booth to the pumps in all weathers. There was no overhead canopy under which they or customers could shelter, because planning permission would not allow their construction in a rural area.

Ray Flack was proprietor of the garage from 1964 until 1973, when the petrol forecourt was taken over by *Total* and the showroom became the agent for selling *Skoda* cars. Ray then moved into a purpose-built workshop at the back of the site. In 1976, he moved into a smaller workshop, on his own land, and continued car repairs until as late as 1995.

Many local youngsters started their working life in either the garage or the café, while lots of people bought their first car from 'Mr Flack'. Three apprentices (John Peters, Brian Chiverton and Barry Hutchins) learned their trade at **Greatham**. It is not unusual, even today, for someone to approach Ray and say, *"I bought a car from your place, years ago"*. Indeed, just this year (2007), one of his neighbours met someone on a mid-Atlantic cruise, who worked in the garage office 40 years ago! She remembered Ray and his family and they remembered her.

*(Having arrived in the village myself at the end of October 1967, I managed to 'write off' my first car within a matter of weeks! Needing a vehicle right away, in order to get into work each day, I recall turning to Ray Flack at **Greatham** Motors and purchasing an old 1952 Morris Minor at a very reasonable price. It had one of the old side-valve engines, a split front windscreen and was painted a very fashionable black! We christened her 'Betsy' and she used to chug along in her own inimitable way, though refusing to go up hills such as Butser and*

the one up to Hawkley! I recall that one of the attendants to serve me petrol was a lady called Pearl, who I later found out was the sister of old friend Bill Marie. Ed.)

A Mr & Mrs Lazarenko managed the garage during the early 1970s and their son, Cliff, later became a famous darts player, learning his skills in *'The Queen'* public house, located just across the road, while waiting for his mum and dad to finish work (see footnote).

The garage finally closed in 1995 and the 'Todmore' estate of private houses was built on the site. Upon their arrival in **Greatham**, Pat and Ray Flack first lived in Todmore Cottage, but then later moved into Elm Villa. Having lived previously in Chalfont St Peter, Buckinghamshire, they re-named the house 'Chalfont' and that name survives today. The cottage was demolished as part of the Todmore development and the Flack's present house, No.1 Todmore, is literally just a few yards from their original cottage home.

Footnote

Cliff Lazarenko (born March 16, 1952) is an English professional darts player, who competed for the British Darts Organisation and the Professional Darts Corporation. Nicknamed 'Big Cliff', he is well known for being a very colourful character, both on and off the stage. He made his first TV appearance on the 1970s television show Indoor League. He then went on to light up the darting circuit, winning numerous titles in both singles and pairs events. He is a four-time World Championship semi-finalist. In 1980, he lost out to Bobby George; the next year he gained revenge on George, by beating him in the quarter-finals, eventually losing to world champion Eric Bristow.

Cliff has being suffering from ill health over the past 12 months, and has now lost a great deal of weight. Because of his illness, he no longer took part in tournaments. However, in the 2007 UK Open Darts at the Reebok Stadium in Bolton, he made a welcome return to the big stage, winning two matches in one night, en route to the second round. He then won another game the next night, before finally falling in the third round.

Greatham Filling Station late 1960s

Greatham Memories

This was a busy filling station, even after the cafe had been demolished

Chapter 21
Huguette and Ray Jenkinson

Rainford 'Ray' Jenkinson
3 May 1932 – 22 January 2007

Ecclesiastes 3:1-11, reading by Rev Michael Ryall

1 'To every thing there is a season and a time to every purpose under the heaven:
2 A time to be born and a time to die; a time to plant and a time to pick up that which is planted;
3 A time to kill and a time to heal; a time to break down and a time to build up;
4 A time to weep and a time to laugh; a time to mourn and a time to dance;
5 A time to cast away stones and a time to gather stones together; a time to embrace and a time to refrain from embracing;
6 A time to get and a time to lose; a time to keep and a time to cast away;
7 A time to rend and a time to sew; a time to keep silence and a time to speak;
8 A time to love and a time to hate; a time of war and a time of peace;
9 What profit hath he that worketh in that wherein he laboureth?
10 I have seen the travail, which God hath given to the sons of men to be exercised in it.
11 He hath made everything beautiful in his time; also he hath set the world in their heart, so that no man can find out the work that God maketh from the beginning to the end.'

Address by Rev Canon Paul Duffet

The reading *(see above)* we have just heard was chosen because it describes Ray's spirituality very well. The way he accepted his illness, and lived creatively within it for over five years, fits the philosophy of Ecclesiastes. Indeed, if Ray had a coat of arms, it would have had as its motto *"There is nothing better for men than to be happy and do good while they live"*.

Ray was born in 1932 in the hamlet of Easthamstead, Berkshire, where his father was a nurse for children with disabilities. He went to Sunday School at the church next door to their home and joined the choir. At the age of sixteen, he went to join the Army Apprentices' School, not too far away at Arborfield. It was here that he trained as a Draughtsman and became confirmed into the church. Upon gaining his apprenticeship, Ray went to serve with the Royal Engineers for the next twenty-four years, gaining the rank of Warrant Officer Class 1. He was offered a commission but refused it, on the grounds that he didn't want to become a 'pen-pusher in an office'.

Serving as a soldier meant travelling, firstly to Germany and then back to Chatham, Kent. It was here that Ray met Huguette, then a student nurse, at a Christmas party. They were eventually married at Holy Trinity Church, Bracknell, to where Ray's parents had moved, on March 2nd 1957. Ray took his 'Clerk of Works' course at Chatham, then held that very post here at Longmoor, before spending a whole year on Christmas Island in the Pacific Ocean. The tour should have been for only six months, but with nobody suitable to replace him, Ray stayed on. He returned to Longmoor, but was soon on his travels once more, firstly to Bahrain and then to Malta in 1963, where he was in charge of the workshops.

Just before that move, Ray and Huguette had bought a plot of land in **Greatham** and, in 1967, he built the house, main drainage and all, mainly by himself, but with Huguette as a willing helper. Back in England, Ray was seconded to the Ministry of Public Building & Works, under whose jurisdiction he supervised the building of HM Prison at Bisley, some married quarters at RAF Odiham and a Post Office in Alton. This was followed by a posting to 'SHAPE' (Supreme Headquarters, Allied Powers in Europe) in Belgium for three years (1968-71), from where he travelled home for a 'long weekend' once every month. Ray's final posting was down to Marchwood, on the coast near Southampton, and he retired from the Army in 1972.

His first civilian appointment was as Deputy Engineer at St Thomas's Hospital in London, where he trained others in the Maintenance Department. Whilst there, he wrote an article for the Hospital Engineer's Magazine, and the editor was so impressed that he had it translated into several languages for publication in Europe. Ray wasn't too happy with the working of the National Health Service and decided to leave. As a result of a course at Keele University, in Staffordshire, Ray was advised to take up teaching and this led to his appointment as a Lecturer at the School of Electrical and Mechanical Engineering at Bordon. He worked there until taking early retirement in 1992, in order to follow his lifelong passion for building miniature steam engines.

Despite the fact that the presence of six such engines in his workshop illustrates his love of this work, he also found time to pursue another favourite pastime. This was to play the piano, which he had learned as a child. When we asked whether he could teach our own children, this eventually turned into almost a full-time job! Indeed, one of his pupils played for the last Christmas Day service in this very church. Ray also found time to join the Liss Brass Band, where he learned to play the cornet. And when the church organist, William Redman, who had played here in *Greatham* for the previous sixty years, became unable to continue, Ray went to the Royal School of Church Music to learn how to play the organ – and continued this for around fifteen years. Indeed, his 'final performance' was at Midnight Mass at Christmas just a few short weeks ago.

Ray was not only a soldier in the Army, but also a 'soldier of Christ'. Wherever he found himself serving, he inevitably sang in the local church choir. Here in *Greatham*, he was a churchwarden for twenty-two years, served terms on the Parochial Church Council both as secretary and treasurer, and also as a member of the Parish Council. He was chairman of the Liphook Modeller's Club right up until December last year, was both a member and treasurer for the Longmoor branch of the Royal Engineers Association. He was also a member of the Arborfield Old Boys' Association.

Ray Jenkinson at the Army Apprentices School c1948

Notwithstanding all that, Ray was a loving husband. He and Huguette formed a special team, as she supported him in every way and everything that he did. He was a loving father and grandfather, and the foster children that he and Huguette cared for have testified to his love for them too. Let us not forget his formidable vegetable garden and the excellent wines that he made, which provided excellent evenings of entertainment at fund-raising and wine-tasting parties. Sometime last year, Ray showed us a cross, made in his own workshop, which he carried with him always. That cross was dear to Ray – the centre of his faith in God. Above all, it was the empty cross he put his trust in, that of Jesus. The Christ and Son of God had suffered too, but had been raised, a victor over all of life's vicissitudes, now the glorified Lord and Saviour of humankind.

That is what Ray would wish you and I to hold onto as well and, in his memory, to join the ranks of the 'Army of Christ'.

*(The above passages are adapted from the funeral service held at St John the Baptist Church, **Greatham**, on Monday 29th January 2007. Paul Duffet had been Rector of **Greatham** between 1980 and 1988, and he kindly handed over his notes to me after the service. I hope I have translated them as closely as possible to their original meaning. Pete Gripton.)*

Huguette's story

As her name would suggest, Huguette was born and raised in France, spending her childhood days living in the dangerous period of German occupation during the Second World War. Indeed, her family lived through hard times, as her father was imprisoned for his being a member of the French resistance. Despite this, Huguette recalls that living in the countryside brought her a good and healthy childhood. After the war, at the age of twelve, she was sent away to boarding school and lived what she recalls as 'a Spartan life', where comfort was certainly not a priority! There was no running water and, at lunchtimes, water was collected from a well and distributed by jug and bowl for drinking and washing. The water was often frozen during winter months and there was no heating in the dormitory, but Hugette insists that it was fun – most of the time!

In March 1954, aged around eighteen, Hugette came to England to improve her English, with the intention that she would return to France a few years later as an English teacher. Applying for work, she was offered a post at a psychiatric hospital at Wallingford, located on the River Thames between Reading and Oxford, but none too certain of what the work would be. After a few weeks she realised that, if she became a student nurse, this would have the advantage of extra English lessons, access to certain colleges in Oxford, and the possibility of gaining some nursing qualifications. At that time, foreigners were still classed as 'aliens', and Huguette had to report to the local police station every six months, to verify that her permit to stay and work had not expired.

It was during this period that Huguette met Ray, at a Christmas party in 1955. She readily admits that, for her, it was not 'love at first sight' – but that Ray came with the one in-built asset of proudly owning his own car, which she thinks was a *Jaguar SS*! This asset obviously carried some weight, as the couple married in 1957, when Ray was on a course at Chatham. Very kindly, the Army gave him the Friday off, that being the day before the wedding – but he still had to be back in the classroom on Monday morning! For the first six months of married life they lived in a rented flat in nearby Gillingham. When the course ended, Ray's posting was to Longmoor Camp and the couple then lived in part of a large house at Tilford, in what was then called by the Army 'a hiring'. It was there, during an almost six-year tenure, that Ray spent a whole year on Christmas Island and another six months in Bahrain. But he did spend time at home too, and Huguette quickly learned how to cope, first with one child, then later with two!

In 1963, Huguette and Ray bought the plot of land in **Greatham**, on which they eventually built their permanent home, just before the whole family decamped to Malta for three years. Whilst on that George Cross island, Huguette started to inquire about teaching again, as this had always been her intended vocation.

After a period of studies in Malta and then a return to England, Huguette was fortunate in finding some work as a supply teacher, followed by classes for adults at a language centre in Haslemere. She also worked in Further Education at local schools, something she had always hoped to do. The Church had always played a large part in her life and, in Malta, she had often helped with Sunday school. Thus, when the Sunday school teacher in *Greatham* left the post, it was Huguette who took over from him. However, she found this still wasn't exactly what she wanted, feeling an overwhelming desire to take a positive direction. After much soul searching, prayer and advice, it was recommended that she begin training as a lay teacher for the Church. After three years of intensive study, Huguette was admitted and licensed as Diocesan Reader by the Bishop of Portsmouth.

Two years later, the incumbent Rector in *Greatham*, Paul Duffett, moved to a new parish and, at the same time, the Diocese found itself under pastoral reorganisation. As a result, *Greatham* became part of the United Benefice that still exists today, the Rector actually living in Hawkley. Thus it was that, in 1988, Huguette became the Church presence in the village, enjoying every part of the ministry that was entrusted to her. In fact, it became a full-time job for her and she was ably supported by Ray, who was Churchwarden at the time, as well as by the local congregation. There were to be many moments of both great joy and deep sorrow, which Huguette shared with her parishioners, and she felt privileged to serve God and the Church in this way.

Apart from all this, Huguette busied herself in many different outlets, such as the Guild of St Helena and the *Greatham* French Circle, both of which were sadly forced to close in later years. There were also the fund-raising activities that she and Ray ran on behalf of the Church and Village Hall – curry evenings, Mothering Sunday lunches, coffee mornings and the famous Amedee cheese and wine evenings. Huguette will always be grateful for the support she received from stalwart helpers, Elsie Collins and Amy Pickard. As if this wasn't enough, Huguette also found the 'spare time', at various periods, to serve as a school governor, parish councillor and carriage driver – she even had her own pony and all the necessary equipment!

At the age of seventy, Huguette finally retired as Diocesan Reader in 2005 and returned to her self-created garden, a source of much satisfaction to her over many years. Sadly, Ray's ill-health came along, followed by his passing away early

*Hugette and Ray married at **Greatham** in March 1967*

in 2007. Huguette has decided to now move closer to her children up in Cambridgeshire and hopes to complete her move later this same year.

A personal view

At one time, there were three ex-Arborfield Apprentice boys living in *Greatham* – Ray Jenkinson, Mike Haben and myself. Sadly, and to coin a phrase, I'm now *'the only ex-boy in the village'*. Mike died last year (2006) and I was able to provide some written tribute to him in the Arborfield Old Boys' Association (AOBA) Newsletter. Now I have the sad duty of penning a few words about Ray, who died in hospital on January 22nd 2007 after a prolonged battle against illness. Despite looking desperately ill for some time previously, Ray made a great effort to attend his last Arborfield Reunion in 2006, accompanied by his wife Huguette.

I first met Ray many years ago, as we were both then on the permanent teaching staff at the School of Electrical and Mechanical Engineering (SEME), Bordon, where Ray was a well-respected lecturer in the Engineering Science Department. A quiet and unassuming man, it was to be quite some time before I found out that he was a fellow ex-Arborfield boy, who had joined up in 1948. Both Ray and Huguette were popular and hard-working members of the local St John the Baptist Church here in *Greatham*, where Ray regularly played the Sunday service organ music and Huguette eventually became the lay preacher. Ray also gave piano lessons from home and enjoyed dabbling in the building and restoration of miniature steam engines. It also became the custom in the village that Ray and Huguette would hold an annual 'cheese and wine' party at their home, the 'takings' being mainly donated to church funds.

It was only a few years ago that I finally persuaded Ray to re-join the AOBA but, once he had done so, he was delighted to meet up with old friends again and to attend several reunions. He also supplied me with a few notes on his earlier experiences, which were published as a 'letter to the editor' in a Newsletter in 2003. One of his favourite memories had been his visit to the Festival of Britain in 1951, just prior to leaving boys' school. Some time ago, he and Huguette attended another reunion, this one for personnel who had been posted to and served on Christmas Island, that must have been during the Fifties. I asked him to write about this chapter of his life and I know he was working on the story until his illness finally began to take its toll. However, Huguette has promised me that she will let me have his notes in due course, in the hope that I may be able to produce something suitable for publication in the future.

Fittingly, Ray's funeral service was held at the village church in *Greatham* on Monday, January 29th. Not surprisingly, the church was packed to the rafters. Rest in peace old friend.

Chapter 22
The Leggett Legacy

One fine evening early in June 2005, Bill Marie rang my doorbell and stood there holding a wad of books and pamphlets. He explained that, since his recent retirement, he had been helping out at an antiques shop over in Grayshott. There, he had come across a small history book published on behalf of the Bramshott and Liphook Preservation Society, that gave a brief history of the Canadian Forces that had been present in that area at the time of both World Wars. *('Liphook, Bramshott and the Canadians' by L.C. Giles, published 1986.)* Upon reading the book, Bill had come across the name 'Leggett' and wondered if this was the same family of whom I had written in my own book ***'A History of Greatham'***.

If I may quote the particular paragraph, which refers to events during the First World War, it reads:

"Canadian Ordnance 'set up shop' at the disused Grigg's Green Brickworks site (opposite Westlands Farm), using all the old sheds and two canvas stores. Canadian Forestry units established a sawmill on the Longmoor Road; the Military Railway carried the timber to and from the mill; the Deer's Hut pub became the Officers' Mess and the Leggetts made part of Grove House (next to Woolmer Gate) available for 'a soldiers' room'."

I then had to go back to my own book and check the words of Joe Leggett, who had written an account of his early childhood days, firstly whilst living at Benham's Lane in **Greatham**, and then later at Grigg's Green, up towards Liphook. Towards the end of his story, Joe recounted the following:

"Unfortunately, Benham's was no longer large enough to meet growing demands. There was despondency once more in the family, at the mere thought of ever moving away from that place which had provided so much happiness. However, 'feelers' had been put out and results were coming in. My parents found themselves in a dilemma as to which premises to choose, and at last decided to look at the latest offer of Grove House, a gentleman's residence in Forest Lane, Grigg's Green.

This was an eight-roomed red brick house, built in 1907, standing in an acre and a half of ground, with a large paddock in the background. Next to the house was a long brick building, consisting of an outside toilet, fuel shed, coach-house, stables for four horses, as well as a harness room. All current 'mod cons' were installed. One look at the place and it was theirs – for an all-inclusive rent of eight shillings and sixpence a week (42½ pence in present day currency)."

I think readers will agree that the two 'Leggett' references, in particular the name 'Grove House', definitely identify the same family and I am pleased to add this little footnote to the original tale of Joe Leggett. Thank you Bill, for being so alert – I have the feeling that there is still a tale to be told of 'what happened next'!

Towards the end of that same year, 2005, I received a letter asking if I would consider making a 'history presentation' to the Liphook Historical group. I was happy to agree to this and started putting some notes together. Prior to the presentation, I went up to Liphook to meet the group's Chairman, Hugh Spratt. We got to talking about the theme of my lecture and I mentioned the 'Joe Leggett' connection. To my surprise and pleasure, he then told me that the Leggett family had been well publicised in Liphook, via a couple of small books that had been written, again on behalf of the Bramshott and Liphook Preservation Society.

When I actually attended Liphook Village Hall to make my presentation, Hugh kindly gave me the two books in question. Both were based upon Joe Leggett's early life, mainly at Grigg's Green, and edited by Ellie Foster. This was the same lady who had given me Joe's original typed notes, upon which I based my chapter in **'A History of Greatham'**. Thus the Joe Leggett episode seems to have turned full circle – and I am glad to have played my own small part in publishing Joe's memoirs. (The titles of the books are *'Growing up in Grigg's Green'* and *'No toys for the boys'*, both of which are available through local outlets in Liphook.)

Chapter 23
Shirley and Pat Redpath

On Wednesday 10th August 2005, the final page was turned on a sad, though most inspiring, paragraph in the story of a popular couple, Shirley and Pat (short for Patrick) Redpath. Many villagers will recall that the Redpaths had lived at No.3 Broadleigh Cottages in **Greatham** for a good number of years, before being involved in a very tragic road accident in late October 2000. This occurred while they were driving home, from a visit to see some relatives in Godalming, during a tremendous storm with heavy rain. In a horrific event, a huge tree was brought down by high winds and crashed down onto their car on the A3, just south of the Hindhead traffic-lights, and they were both severely injured. Sadly, Pat failed to survive his injuries and was buried at **Greatham Church** on November 24th that same year.

Shirley meanwhile was in a life-threatening condition and, at first, unaware of Pat's fate. I think she was first treated at a hospital in Worthing, down on the Sussex coast, before being transferred to the spinal injuries unit at Oddstock Hospital in Salisbury, Wiltshire. Fate decreed that Shirley had been so badly injured that she faced the remainder of her life in a wheelchair, paralysed from the neck downwards. It was around this time that my wife Joyce and I, along with our good friends Helen and Tim Gould from Snailing Lane, went down to visit her. I must admit that I was somewhat concerned about the visit – would Shirley be glad to see us in her condition; and would she be able to put up with a visit? At least, I thought, with the four of us all going there together, we'd be able to keep some sort of conversation going for a short while. Happily, all my fears were completely unfounded. Despite her injuries and the loss of husband Pat, Shirley was an inspiration to us all. She was so full of life and determined not to be beaten by her confinement and immobility. Most of the conversation was down to her, as she asked about what we were doing and what was going on in the village, eager to put us at our ease.

Pat Redpath (right) spent some time serving with the RAF

Later, Shirley was transferred to the Holy Cross Hospital at Haslemere, which made visits easier and more localised for her many friends and loving family. I'm sure that those visits made by all of her relatives were the thing that kept Shirley going, she lived for her family. We, her friends and acquaintances of long standing, generally visited as a foursome and eventually, when Shirley was able to leave the hospital on trips and visits, it would take the four of us to attach the wheelchair safely into the specially adapted van that was essential to Shirley's mobility. She used to laugh as we struggled to put the brakes on and attach the seat belts to keep the wheelchair stationary within the van, saying *"I thought you'd have worked it out by now!"* I remember us taking her to the cinema a couple of times and one memorable trip out was to Marwell Zoo, down near Winchester, when we had a lovely day together.

After a while, Shirley was able to move into her own specially-adapted accommodation, sharing a home with her daughter Julie (Lockley) and family, down at Cowplain. It was here that we continued to visit her on occasion, as well as other close friends from her *Greatham* days. Those that I know included Jackie and Bill Marie, Sandra and Tony Allan, and Jo and John Keep. Apologies for any names I've not known about! The one great fear was that, when Shirley caught an infection, she would be unable to fight it off due to her paralysis. Sadly, having previously fought off a few such attacks with her inner strength and fortitude, this finally proved to be the case and our dear friend finally succumbed to a chest infection at the beginning of August.

One thing that can be safely said is that Shirley was surrounded by love and affection, during those last few years of her life. I know that we only saw her occasionally, but visits by her close family members were, I'm sure, virtually a daily occurrence – and of course Julie and husband Mark were always close at hand. Shirley leaves two children, that's Julie and her elder brother – also Mark – as well as their spouses and lovely children. But she also leaves behind some wonderful memories of a very special lady.

Earlier days

At Shirley's funeral service, held in a packed St John the Baptist Church in *Greatham*, it was left to her brother Peter to pay tribute to his sister. He did this by reporting the main facts of her life, mixed with a few personal anecdotes that raised some smiles and tears. Shirley Joan Mills was born at Godalming, Surrey, on the 20th December 1941, a sister to John. By January 1949, another four brothers and a sister had arrived on the scene. At school, Shirley excelled, and would possibly have gone on to great things on an educational side. She also proved to be good at sports, with a particular fondness for netball.

But her Dad died in 1956 and Shirley took on the challenge of helping her mother to run the home and family affairs. Then, in 1963, her family noticed a change in Shirley, when she met up with Patrick Redpath, known to all as Pat. It was obviously a case of 'true love' and the happy couple were married on April 4th 1964 and took up residence at their home in *Greatham*, up on the old A325 that ran through the middle of the village. They were to reside there for thirty-six years, bringing first a son, Mark, then a daughter, Julie, into the world. And, of course, they joined in the daily rhythm of village life and made new friends.

Our own relationship with the Redpaths probably started in the early 1970s, when my wife Joyce started to play netball for a local team, known as *'The Jays'*. Shirley was another member of that team, along with Jackie Marie and Helen Gould, and the four 'girls' began their long-lasting friendship, which obviously soon began to include the four 'boys' - myself, Pat, Tim and Bill. At one stage, we eight used to meet up at one house or another and play a few hands of Canasta. But with families growing up and expanding, it was inevitable that these get-togethers reached a natural conclusion and it was then usually left to 'special events' to bring us together.

I recall one particular 'special event' very well; it must have been Pat's 60th birthday, for which a 'party' was held at his mother's house in 1993. The house lay on the other side of the 'old' A3 up at Rake and had once been an old coaching inn. While we were there, Pat showed us a book with a tale of how some 'revenue men' had once captured a smuggler and taken him down into the cellar of the inn and beaten him to death. He also showed us around the upstairs of the house, which had very low ceilings and narrow corridors. There was a 'ghostly' side to it all too, when Pat told us that no matter how closely his mother shut the bedroom doors every night, they were always all wide open the following morning! True or not, the tale certainly brought a few goose bumps to the back of one's neck!

If I remember correctly, at some time in the early 1980s, Shirley and Pat took over the running of a local printing firm at Liss, but ill health brought that episode to an unfortunate conclusion and Pat then took up painting and decorating for a living. Upon a return from Australia in the early days of January 1997, Joyce and I found that a burst pipe in our loft had caused substantial flooding and pretty well wiped out our front bedroom and kitchen – the ceilings in particular! It was thanks to Pat that new ceilings and re-decoration brought the house quickly back to normality. In the meantime, Shirley had taken up a secretarial post at *Blacknest Golf Club*. Both of them took up the game of bowls, along with good friends Jackie and Bill, and the foursome became members of the club at nearby Liphook.

During 1996, the new A3 dual-carriageway had opened to the south of **Greatham** and, unfortunately, life then became somewhat less comfortable for Pat and Shirley, as the road past their front door became busier on an almost daily basis. I recall Pat telling me that it was difficult to back his van into the road some mornings.

Returning now to Shirley's funeral service, Sandra Allan made the journey to **Greatham** with husband Tony, following their recent move to Swanage, down on the lovely Dorset coast. Sandra read the following words of comfort - I am not sure as to the author, but I feel that they are well worth repeating here:

"Death is nothing at all. I have only slipped into the next room. I am I and you are you. Whatever we were to each other, that we still are. Call me by my old familiar name; speak to me in the same easy way, which you always used. Put no difference in your tone; wear no forced air of solemnity or sorrow. Laugh as we always laughed at the little jokes that we shared together. Let my name be ever the household word that it always was; let it be spoken without effort, without the trace of a shadow on it. Life means all that it ever meant. It is the same as it ever was; there is unbroken continuity. Why should I be out of mind because I am out of sight? I am waiting for you, for an interval, somewhere very near, just around the corner."

Following the interment, many faces, both new and familiar to me, were to be seen around the Church. One belonged to Janet Ransome, who I hadn't seen for many a long year, since she used to be in the same netball team as Shirley and the other girls. It must have been heartening for the family that so many old friends turned up to pay tribute to Shirley and to show their love and affection. Shirley and Pat are now joined together in death, as they were so strongly in life.

(Just changing the subject slightly, but only a few villagers may know that Shirley's brother Michael is the now retired footballer 'Mick' Mills, who played for Ipswich and Southampton, as well as going on to become an international star of the England team. I can still remember the last time that I saw Mick playing 'live', when his then team Southampton lost an FA Cup semi-final to my own side Everton, that match taking place at Arsenal's Highbury Stadium back in 1984. I have bumped into Mick on occasion since then, probably whilst he was visiting Shirley in hospital, but I've never got around to 'rubbing it in'! Ed.)

Chapter 24
Hampshire Heathland Project (HHP)

Longmoor Inclosure is a very important heathland site, being home to many rare animals and plants, including birds such as the Dartford Warbler. Over time, pine and birch trees invade the open heathland and form areas of scrub that are very poor for wildlife. During 2003 and onwards, the HHP, in partnership with the Ministry of Defence (MoD), aimed to restore the open areas of heathland for the benefit of the wildlife and visitors to Longmoor Inclosure. This involved the removal of many trees that had grown over former heathland.

In July of 2004, notices began to appear around the range area under the heading of *"Cattle grazing at Longmoor Army Training Area"* and were worded as shown below.

My wife Joyce and I use the heathland on either side of the main A3 trunk road as often as time and 'red flags' allow. It can certainly be confirmed that the cattle have been grazing the area to the north of **Greatham** for some months now – though it is difficult for the amateur viewer to see what effect they are having. The other visible evidence of the return to heathland is the number of old pine trees that have been removed, in large areas both north and south of the village. While it is sad to see the disappearance of these trees, it certainly opens up extensive views across the heath that were invisible before, so the long-term advantages of the tree clearance are becoming clear.

Background
The Longmoor army training area supports an important range of lowland heathland habitats and associated species. The area is protected under UK and European law by a number of conservation designations. You will probably have noticed the recent tree and scrub clearance undertaken on the heath by the MoD, in partnership with the HHP. This work has made the initial step towards the joint MoD and English Nature target to improve the condition of the site. Cattle will begin grazing the site in spring 2005, in order to help the diversity of heathland habitats to recover. The proposals have been drawn up by MoD and HHP, in consultation with a number of bodies, including the Longmoor Conservation Group, the local parish, town and district councils.

Changes to the site
(referring to an accompanying map)
Public access in these areas will be permitted as normal during range closure times.
The erection of the fence is due to take place in September 2004 (which it did!)
An initial introduction of approximately twelve cattle will take place in spring 2005. It is proposed that the cattle will be on site for spring and summer months from 2005 onwards.
The cattle will be checked daily by the stock manager and contact details provided in case of emergency.

Chapter 25
Greatham Inn

On the evening of Thursday 13th May 2004, the newly resurrected public house, originally known for many years as *'The Queen'*, opened its doors as *'The Greatham Inn'*. It had been a sad day for the village when the old pub had closed down during 2001, to be followed the next year by closure of the other village hostelry, *'The Silver Birch'*. Following protracted battles against planning applications and orders in relation to both locations, a plan was put forward to refurbish at least one of the two closed premises and it was *'The Silver Birch'* (formerly *'The Woolmer Hotel'*) that lost out. Thus it was that, at 6.30 p.m. on that Thursday that landlord Alan Maxwell was able to declare *'The Greatham Inn'* officially open, offering *"Real ales and the most fabulous feasting, served each day until late"*, as it says on the notice-board.

During the Summer of 2006, the northern half of the **Greatham Inn's** car-park began to be converted into a building site, on which four houses are to be constructed. From the small sizes of the plots, it would appear that these may possibly be 'starter homes' for first-time buyers. Then, during the first few days of October, work finally looked as if it was starting on the development at the old *Silver Birch* site, where a number of houses are to be located. There are virtually no amenities in the village to support either of these plans, but at least the *Silver Birch* site will provide a better sight than that of the past few years - a derelict building, where once so much enjoyment was 'on tap'.

*The **Greatham Inn** today.*

Peter Gripton

Chapter 26
The Carylls

The alabaster tomb of Dame Margery Caryl

In the Sussex village of South Harting, nestling just beneath the hills of the South Downs, lies the Church of St Mary and St Gabriel, conspicuously situated beneath its fine green spire. Hidden away in its south transept is the battered effigy of Sir Richard Caryll, who died in the mediaeval year of 1616. The Carylls were a Catholic family who owned large tracts of land in Sussex but, despite their faith, built a mortuary chapel adjoining the chancel of Harting Church. Sir Richard it was who married Margery, daughter of Elizabeth and John Freeland of **Greatham**. And it is the alabaster tomb of the same Dame Margery Caryll that still reposes in the ruined old St John's Church here in **Greatham**.

*The ruins of **Greatham's** old church still a village highlight*

Peter Gripton

Epilogue

Having now completed this second (and rather unexpected) book about **Greatham**, perhaps it is now time to give the old keyboard a well-earned rest! It is amazing to see the changes in the village in the short four years or so since *'A History of Greatham'* was published, such as the sad deaths of so many friends and neighbours, and the closure of one of the two village pubs. But of course history moves on so rapidly, it is difficult to keep up with the times one lives in, never mind those times long passed. But I hope this book enables people to once again take a 'peep into the past' and enjoy the stories within.

My thanks go to all who contributed, I do hope I haven't missed anyone out from my list of acknowledgements. Thanks also and again to Ken Anderson, old Arborfield and Army colleague, who has kindly and expertly put together my scribbled efforts these past few months and turned them into the presentation you see in front of you - any errors are entirely down to me. When I look back at the *'Introduction'* to my first book, I see that this writing epidemic of mine all derived from that *'Village Appraisal'* meeting in March 1998, which is almost ten years ago. So yes, it is time to turn the final page.

Pete Gripton, 2008

Appendix A
Le Court occupants

BUTLER

Butler, William esq.	Farmer		1847
	Le Court		1855
	Le Court		1857
William Eldridge	Le Court		1859

FOSTER
Foster, Sampson esq.	Le Court (assumed)		1871
Foster, William Fry	Le Court		1875
			1878
			1880

SANDFORD

Sandford, Mrs.	Le Court		1885
			1889

HARRISON

Harrison, Heath esq., JP	Le Court		1895
			1903
			1907
(Alexander, William	Gardener to H. Harrison)		1907
Harrison, Heath esq., JP			1911
(Alexander, William	Gardener to H. Harrison)		1911
Harrison, Heath esq., JP			1915
(Peskett, John A	Gardener to H. Harrison)		1915
Harrison, Sir Heath Bart, JP			1920
(Carr, Edward E	Gardener to Sir Heath)		1920
Harrison, Sir Heath Bart, JP			1923
(Carr, Edward E	Gardener) (assumed)		1923
Harrison, Sir Heath Bart, JP			1927
(Carr, Edward E	Gardener)		1927
(Fry, Stephen	Gamekeeper to Sir Heath)		1927
Harrison, Sir Heath Bart, JP			1931
(Carr, Edward E	Gardener to Sir Heath)		1931
(Fry, Stephen	Gamekeeper)		1931
Harrison, Lady	Le Court		1935
(Fry, Stephen	Gamekeeper to Lady Harrison)		1935

KNIGHT

Knight, Brig.-Gen. Henry L, DSO	Le Court		1939

Appendix B
Lords of the Manor / Manor House occupants

THE CHAWNERS

Chawner, Henry	Lord of the manor	1847
Chawner, Capt EH	Lord of the manor	1855
	(assumed)	1857
	(of Newton Valence)	1859
		1871
		1875
(Ewen, Mrs Elizabeth	Manor House)	1875
Chawner, Capt EH	Lord of the manor, Liss Place	1878
(Ewen, Mrs Elizabeth	Manor House)	1878
Chawner, Capt EH	Lord of the manor, Liss Place	1880
(Ewen, Mrs Elizabeth	Manor House)	1880

THE CORYTONS

Coryton, George Edward, JP	Lord of the manor, Liss Place	1885
Coryton, Frederick, JP, MFH	Lord of the manor, Liss Place	1889
		1895
(Unwin, Mrs	Manor House)	1895
Coryton, Frederick JP, MFH	Lord of the manor, Manor House	1903
		1907
		1911
		1915
		1920
		1923
Coryton, Augustus Fred'k JP	Lord of the manor, Manor House	1927
		1931
Coryton, Augustus Fred'k JP	Lord of the manor, Gold's House	1935
(Coryton, Miss Isolda	Manor House)	1935
Coryton, Capt. AF, JP	Manor House	1939
(Coryton, Miss Isolda	Gold's House)	1939

Appendix C
Pubs & Hotels

The Queen

Wells, George	Innkeeper	1871
	Queen's Head, shopkeeper & farmer	1875
	Farmer, shopkeeper & victualler, Queen's Head	1878
	Queen's Head, shopkeeper & farmer	1880
Knight, John	Queen's Head PH & shopkeeper	1885
Davis, Samson	Queen's Head PH & shopkeeper	1889
		1895
	The Queen's PH & shopkeeper, Refreshment contractor to Longmoor Camp, ale & stout merchant	1903
	Queen Inn, Greatham, proprietor, Wine & spirit merchant	1907L
Davis, Samson	Apartments, Kingshott Villas	1907B
Hopkins, Henry Herbert	Grocer & The Queen PH	1907
Kemp, Martin	The Queen PH	1911
Goddard, John	The Queen PH	1915
		1920
		1923
Rixon, Harry	The Queen PH	1927
	TN Blackmoor 12	1931
		1935
	TN Blackmoor 212	1939

The Woolmer Hotel

Pearson, Fred William	Woolmer Hotel	1903B
Garner, Thomas	Woolmer Hotel & jobmaster	1907B
Hedley, Mrs Drusilla	Woolmer Hotel	1923B
Smith, Mrs S	Woolmer Hotel	1927B
Roy, Mrs Jean	Woolmer Hotel, prop	1931B
	TN Blackmoor 2	1935B
	TN Blackmoor 262	1939B

'The Queen' public house in days gone by

Index

A
Adlam, Lt Col 'Tommy' 5
Allan, Sandra 30, 83
Allan, Tony 82
Allotments 68
Alresford 8
Alton 8
Arborfield Old Boys' Association 75, 78
Armitage, Susan 31
Army Apprentices School 75, 97

B
Baker's Field 20
Bandford, Pat 44
Bather, The 33
Beckford, Francis Love 65
Bedales School 5
Beeleigh 32
Beenham, Chris 35, 36
Benham's Lane 4, 22, 23, 41, 79
Blackmoor Church 6, 48
Blackmoor Estate 4
Blackwell, Caroline 36, 60
Blanchard, Mary 1
Bolam, Jean 29
Booton Hall 19
Booton, Sue and Alan 18, 48
Bracken Cottage 49
Bramshott and Liphook Preservation Society 80
Brewis, Lady Anne MBE 22
Brewis, Rev John Salisbury 23
Bridger, James 5, 6
Bridger, Olive 4, 8
Broadleigh Cottages 81
Brooker, Gwen 29
Brownies 30, 31, 38
Burma Star 34

C
Caryll, Dame Margery 65, 86
Caryll, Sir Richard 65, 86
Chalmers, Matilda 9
Cheshire Home 32, 62
Chiverton, Brian 71

Church Lane 20, 29, 31, 35, 36, 37, 60, 61, 62, 63
Churcher's College 4, 7
Coffin, Joyce 31
Collins, Elsie 75
Collins, Ernie and Dorothy 31
Collins, Jim 32
Cooke, John 48, 49
Coombes, Betty 29, 30, 31, 32
Coombes, Gilbert 31, 33
Coombes, Jane 29
Coombes, Maurice and Florrie 34
Corps, Thomas 35, 36, 37, 60
Coryton, Augustus Frederick 13, 15, 17
Coryton, Julia 13

D
Dale-Harris, Anna 13
Darby, Fanny 2
Deal Cottages 29, 31, 32, 33, 31
Deal Farm 18, 19, 20, 21, 48, 63
Deal Nap Farm 20
Deer's Hut, The 42
Dinkelmann, Peter 26
Dorcas 32
Dow, Sandra 33
Duffet, Rev Canon Paul 26, 74, 77
Dunn, Brenda 50, 54
Dunn, Jack 50, 51, 52, 55
Dunn, Thomas 51

E
Empshott 1
Evans, Melanie 33

F
Farr, Win 64
Farrar, Shirley 64
Fisher, Julia 13
Flack, Pat 9
Flack, Ray 33, 70, 71
Flander, Mrs 48
Ford, David 2
Ford, George 2
Ford, Michael 1, 24
Ford, William 1, 2

Forestside Farm 1, 2, 4, 24
Forge House 62
Foster, Ellie 78
Foster, James 20
Foster, Joseph 65, 66
Foster, Nigel 65, 66
Foster, Sampson Lloyd 67
Foster, William Fry 67
Freeland, Elizabeth and John 86

G
Gerard, Rita 31
Giffard, William 18
Gilbert, Archibald Henry 48
Gilliatt, Richard 16
Girl Guides 30, 31, 41
Gould, Helen and Tim 81
Goulds House 13
Graves, Elaine and John 46, 47
Greatham Inn 10, 85
Greatham Mill Gardens 31, 46
Greatham School 4, 7, 21, 29, 40, 42, 52, 53
Greatham Service Station 70
Gripton, Joyce 31
Grove House 79

H
Haben, Mike 78
Hampshire Hog 5, 16
Hangers, The 47
Harrison, Sir Heath 35, 37, 61
Harrow School 16
Hawkley and Liss Choral Societies 4
Hawkley Road 20
Heatley, Reverend David 3
Higgins, Major 58
Hipkis, PC 32
Hiscock, Charles 3
Hiscock, Frederick Charles 21
Home Guard 4, 43, 55, 56
Howard, Tommy and Ivy 50
Humby, Florence 36
Hutchins, Barry 71

J

Jean Turner, Jean 30
Jenkinson, Huguette 32, 50, 76
Jenkinson, Ray 72, 73, 78
John Deere 7
Jones, Stanley 45

K

Keep, Jo and John 82
Keeper's Cottage 35, 36, 60, 35, 37
Kemp, Robert 33
King's Holt Cottage 29, 32
Kingshott Cottages 29
Knott, Winnie 30

L

Lacey, Hazel 45
Lazarenko, Cliff 71
Le Court 32, 35, 61, 62, 65, 66, 67, 68, 90
Lee, Michael QC 13, 17
Leggett, Joe 77
Lewis, Roger 68
Lilley, Shirley 30
Liphook Modeller's Club 73
Liss Brass Band 73
Little Abbey Preparatory School 7
Longmoor Army Camp 8, 24, 33, 42, 43, 51, 57, 60, 76
Longmoor Common 48
Longmoor Military Railway 51
Luff, Alice 31
Luttrell-West, Cecil Francis 26, 48
Lyss Place 16

M

Madgwick, Frank 70
Magdalene College 16
Malcom Workman 45
Manor House 13, 16, 17, 61, 65, 68, 91
Marie, Bill 77, 80
Matthews, Brian 48
Maxwell, Alan 83
McCann, Wendy 18
Medstead 8
Meech, Malcolm and Jean 50
Methodist Church 25
Mid-Hants Railway Company 8
Mill, Greatham 46
Mitchell, Andy 14
Moseley, Bill 43
Murphy, Winifred 64

N

Newlin, Rev Richard 66

P

Palmer, Anne Beatrice Mary 22
Palmer, Roundell 48
Parochial Church Council 4, 6, 75
Peters, John 71
Petersfield Road 3, 29, 70
Philpot, Letitia Frances 67
Pickard, Amy 32, 77
Pilgrim's Way 35
Pook Cottage 29, 31
POWs, German 56
Pumphrey, Captain 31
Pumphrey, Frances 46, 47

Q

Queen's Head 10, 11, 92

R

Randall, Martha and Arthur 31, 33
Ransome, Janet 83
Redman, David 7, 8, 9, 12, 19
Redman, Edgar 3, 8, 45
Redman, Emma Jane 3
Redman, Olive 2, 4, 5, 9, 23, 24
Redman, William 75
Redman, William Albert 3, 8
Redpath, Pat 33, 79
Redpath, Shirley 30, 31, 32, 33, 39, 64, 81, 82, 83
Richards, Barry 16
Robins 35, 37, 60, 61, 62, 61
Robinson, Shirley 30
Roke, Ann and Brian Roke 33
Rolling, Jane 29
Rolling, John 30, 33
Rook's Farm 3, 21
Russell, John 26, 27, 29, 31, 33
Russell, Lisa and Philippa 32
Russell, Simon and Mark 30
Ryall, Rev Michael 74

S

Scott, Jill 48
Selborne, Lord 4, 5, 48
Shepherd, Eileen 40
Shepherd, Gladys 40
Shepherd's Mead 20
Shotter, Dr Ronald 19, 20, 21, 63
Shotter, William 63
Shuttleworth, Violet 17
Sillence, Simon 50
Silver Birch 33, 50, 83
Siney, Alan 29
Siney, Eric 32
Siney, Karen 30
Smith, Frank 42, 45
Snailing Lane 31, 49, 81

Spratt, Hugh 79
St John the Baptist Church 27
St Martin's Church 53
St Mary's Hall 4
St Matthew's Primary School 5
Stamp, Stan 29
Sunday School 32, 39, 74
Sunnyside 49
Swain's Cottage 21, 31, 61, 63
Swatton, Prue 35, 36, 60

T

Tanner's Farm 20
Teague, Mary Ann 2
Tennyson, Lionel 16
Thele Knapp 32
Todmore 10, 69, 71
Tom's Acre Cottage 31
Trigg, Betty 30
Trigg, Fred 31
Trigg, Henry 18, 29, 48
Trigg, Thomas 29
Tyler, Rev R W 4

W

Wain, Charles Jeffery 4, 53
Wakeford, George and Michael 33
Warbler, Dartford 82
Watercress Line 7
Waterhouse, Alfred 48
Weavers, The 64
Webb, George 56
Wells, George 10
Wells, Peter 9
Wells, Ray 10
Wendon, PC 31
Wesley Lodge 64
Wesleyan Chapel 24
Whangerei Fruit Farm 41
White, Rev Gilbert 22
Windibank, Rachael 30
Wolfmere Lane 33
Wolmer, Viscount 18, 22
Women's Institute 6, 64
Woolmer Hotel 7, 41, 44, 85, 92
Workman, Phyllis 38, 45
Wymering Church 55

Other Books by Peter Gripton
or published by Las Atalayas Publishing

The original 'A History of Greatham'
by Peter Gripton

The present-day Parish of Greatham lies in the county of Hampshire, on either side of the old Farnham (Surrey) to Petersfield Turnpike. The 'Domesday Book' of 1086 recorded Greatham as being 'Terra Regis', a Latin term meaning 'Land of the King', indicating that this was once a Royal manor belonging to William the Conqueror himself. In later years, the manor passed through many families by marriage and by purchase, including the Devenish, Marshall, Norton, Freeland, Love, Chawner and Coryton families. The name of the village has changed many times, however slightly, over the years. Greteham, Grietham, Gretham, Grutham, Gratham all derived from two separate words, the 'Old-English' (Anglo-Saxon) 'ham', meaning 'village, estate, manor or homestead' and an old Scandinavian word 'griot' or 'gryt', meaning 'stones or stony ground'. Thus the name 'Greotham' came into being, literally a 'stony estate' or 'farm on gravel'.

196 pages, 8.5" x 11", perfect binding, white interior paper (60# weight), black and white interior ink, white exterior paper (100# weight), full-colour exterior ink

Available through the Internet at www.amazon.co.uk
ISBN 9780955675317

Korea 1950-53 Recounting REME Involvement
by John Dutton

The story of the War in Korea and of the part played by the REME from 1950 to 1953 as told by various individuals of that Corps, makes fascinating reading. The support and devotion to their colleagues is most apparent, but typical of the British soldier, these experiences are balanced with a sense of sympathy for the unfortunate Korean civilian population caught up in the conflict, and it wouldn't be a true story of the British soldier without its sprinkling of 'squaddie' humour. John Dutton has provided an excellent compilation of personal accounts in this comprehensive story of the Royal Electrical and Mechanical Engineers at war where the positioning of Light Aid Detachments and Field Workshops was just as important to senior commanders in their tactical planning as was the medical back-up of a Regimental Aid Post or a Field Ambulance.

236 pages, 6" x 9", jacket-hardcover binding, cream interior paper (50# weight), black and white interior ink, white exterior paper (100# weight), full-colour exterior ink

Available through the Internet at www.amazon.co.uk
ISBN 9780955675300

Collared by God
Written by Paul S Duffett

This book chronicles the life of an ordinary parson from his schooldays through his experiences at College and ordination to then working in his first church in Portsmouth. The recollections of his time spent with the Abanta Bazulu in South Africa make particularly fascinating reading. On returning to the UK he tells of life in the community first in Hampshire and then in a Cambridgeshire village before retiring.

186 pages, 6" x 9", perfect binding, cream interior paper (60# weight), black and white interior ink, white exterior paper (100# weight), full-colour exterior ink.

Available through the Internet at www.amazon.co.uk
ISBN 9780955675331

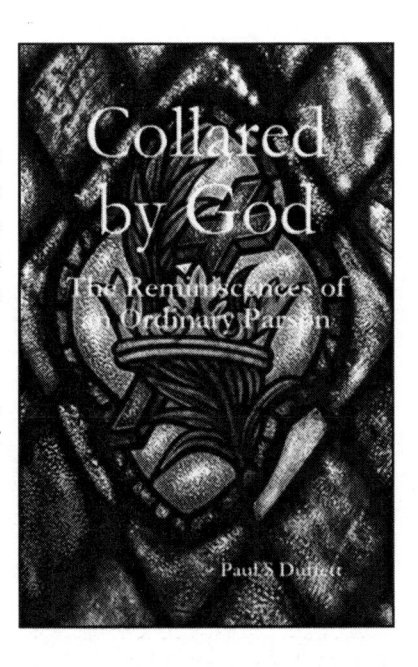

The Arborfield Apprentice by Peter Gripton

This book is an illustrated history of the Arborfield Army Apprentices' School and Colleges. Containing over 500 pages with more than 200 photographs and illustrations it embraces the complete history of Army Apprentice training at Arborfield from 1939 to 2004. As well as being a 'must read' for all who served at Arborfield it is also the most important and authoritive historical work for all those interested in junior soldier tradesman training in the British Army. A supplement covering the final years of the Army Technical Foundation College at Arborfield is also included free of charge with each copy of the book.

This book may be purchased for £18.50 + £7.50 p&p only from
REME Association Shop, The REME Museum of Technology
Isaac Newton Road, Arborfield, Reading, RG2 9NJ.
Tel: 0118 976 3223

ISBN 0954514203

TeeCee's Arborfield Odes by Tony Church

For those who started their Army careers as Army Apprentice Tradesmen at the Army Apprentices School or College at Arborfield they will be well aware that Arborfield has always held a special place in their hearts. TeeCee's collection of amusing and sometimes poignant verses reflects much of the life and attitudes of many who spent their formative years there and this collection of those well deserves a place on their bookshelves.

Printed: 112 pages, 6" x 9", jacket-hardcover binding, cream interior paper (50# weight), black and white interior ink, white exterior paper (100# weight), full-colour exterior ink.

Available through the Internet at www.amazon.co.uk
ISBN 9780955675322